Ancient Arts of the
Americas

NOTRE DAME COLLEGE OF EDUCATION
MOUNT PLEASANT
LIVERPOOL L3 5SP

Ancient Arts of the
Americas

G. H. S. Bushnell

London
Thames and Hudson

© THAMES AND HUDSON 1965

PRINTED IN FRANCE BY INTERGRAPHIC LTD

Contents

Introduction

The Pre-Columbian art of America has left its most conspicuous remains in the areas where the ancient civilizations reached their highest levels, namely Mexico with its southern neighbours, for which I shall use the name Mesoamerica, and Peru. Some branches of it, particularly architecture, have for various reasons left few traces outside these regions, though others, especially pottery and metalwork, were notably successful in parts of Central America and the northern Andes. Of the two main areas, Mesoamerica is superior to Peru in some ways, and notably so in the amount and vigour of its stone sculpture. On the other hand the dry climate of the coast of Peru has allowed the preservation of perishable materials, especially textiles, of which our knowledge in other places is almost entirely dependent on indirect evidence such as carving on stone.

Apart from two isolated instances of uncertain age in Mexico, there is nothing in the New World to compare with the rich Pleistocene art of the Old. These instances are a dog-like animal head carved from the sacrum of an extinct llama found over 80 years ago at Tequixquiac, about 40 miles north of Mexico City, and some confused scratches on a small piece of mammoth bone which are thought to include outlines of a bison, a tapir and some mammoths or mastodons, from Valsequillo, Puebla.

Artistic development in Mexico cannot be said to begin until after the establishment of settled agricultural villages round about 1500 B C. In Peru, sophisticated designs are found on textiles and on some small carved objects in coastal settlements which may date from 500 to 1,000 years earlier. On the coast of Ecuador, well-made monochrome pottery, decorated in various ways, appeared well before 2500 B C, and it was soon followed by a curious type of hand-modelled female figurine.

7

In both Mexico and Peru there was a great step forward when the earliest great religious centres supported by dependent cultivators were developed early in the first millennium B C. It used to be thought that this led up in both areas to an intellectual and artistic climax or period of florescence named the Classic Period, within the first millenium A D. What went before, starting with the first permanent villages in Mexico and with the earliest pottery in Peru, about 1800 B C, has been named the Pre-Classic or Formative Period, and what followed, up to the Spanish Conquest, has been named the Post-Classic Period. This general scheme is still convenient and will be used in this book as a chronological framework for these areas, but it is neither so significant nor of such wide application as we used to believe. It fits the Maya civilization of south-east Mexico and the adjacent areas well, since this had its climax from about A D 300 to 900, but developments which took place in the lowlands of Tabasco on the Gulf Coast roughly a millenium earlier cannot reasonably be called anything but Classic in character. A climax was reached in Peru at about the same time as that of the Maya, say from A D 250 to 750, but it differed considerably in character, and it can justly be claimed that what the art gained at this time in technical perfection it lost in vigour in comparison with an earlier period. In some places, such as western Mexico, it is not possible so far to detect a corresponding Classic stage, and elsewhere, for example in Ecuador and Colombia, different systems of chronology are more suitable.

The production of works of art was distinguished throughout by great manual skill with few mechanical aids. Stone carving, from the great sculptures of Mesoamerica to the most delicate jades, was done with stone and bone tools and abrasives, and hollows and perforations were made with tubular drills of bone or wood and sand. Metal was unknown in Mesoamerica until Post-Classic times, and its introduction had no effect on stone working, but it may have been used for this to some extent in Peru, where hardened copper was known long before. The wheel was, for practical purposes, unknown in any form, and all pottery was made by coiling, hand-modelling, paddle and anvil, or casting

8

in moulds. This did not diminish its quality, but it meant that there was an absence of essentially wheel-made shapes. Textiles of surpassing excellence were made and many examples from the dry Peruvian coast survive in good condition, but the looms were of the simplest, and many processes could have been carried out only by hand.

CHAPTER ONE

Mexico

It has already been said that artistic development in Mexico does not begin until after the establishment of permanent villages, but it is not always possible from the archaeological record to tell whether a village was settled throughout the year or occupied only at certain seasons. The earliest permanent village which we know of in Mexico, at Chiapa de Corzo, Chiapas, was settled between 1500 and 1000 B C, but some sites near Tehuacán in Puebla may prove to be rather earlier. Solid hand-modelled figurines have been found at Chiapa de Corzo, also well-made white and red-and-white pottery bowls and storage jars, but these are rather the forerunners of the art of the Formative Period than works of art in their own right. Somewhat similar assemblages are found at villages such as El Arbolillo and Zacatenco near the great lake which used to fill much of the Valley of Mexico where Mexico City now stands, but these are now thought by some to be rather later in date, from 1000 B C onwards. The figurines found here are of many types, but all are handmade and most of their features are formed by applied fillets of clay, including the 'coffee bean' eyes found on some. They represent women, who may have an elaborate head-dress but no other clothes, and are very numerous. They are thought to have been used in a fertility cult.

OLMEC
The first well-developed art style is found in the lowland region of swamps and tropical jungles on the Gulf Coast, at the southern-most limits of the Bay of Campeche where Tabasco joins Vera-cruz. The name Olmec has come to be applied to both the civi-lization and the art style, although it properly belongs to a people of much later date. The main centre so far known, which may indeed have been the principal shrine, was on a low island surrounded

1 Mask, thought to represent a highly stylized jaguar face, of serpentine blocks, coloured sands and clays. La Venta, Tabasco

by swamps at La Venta. The nucleus of this site is about half a mile long, and there are some outlying ruins which extend it to about 1½ miles. The central area, which has been partly excavated, is aligned along an axis about 8 degrees west of true north. It contains a large pyramid measuring 420 by 240 feet and 100 feet in height, north of which is an elongated court enclosed by low platforms and bounded to the north by a mound. North of this again is another court bounded by low platforms each crowned by a closely-set palisade of natural basaltic columns. Unlike the later stone-faced structures, pyramid and platforms are built of brightly-coloured clays, red, yellow and purple.

This site, with its orderly grouping of great masses of material, gives the keynote to all ancient American architecture, which was always concerned more with external lay-out and the enclosure of space than with the interiors of buildings. If the great pyramid at La Venta and its other mounds or pyramids ever supported any buildings, they must have been of perishable materials and they have left no trace, but even the temples which crowned the most majestic Maya pyramids had small and dark interiors, and not until Post-Classic times were large areas sometimes roofed.

La Venta appears to have been occupied from about 800 to 400 B C, during which time there were four rather extensive recon-

structions, perhaps at 104-year intervals to mark the ends of double
calendar cycles of 52 years, because such 52-year cycles were
important to many of the later peoples and their endings were
marked by the reconstruction and enlargement of their monuments.
Among the features associated with the reconstructions at La
Venta were the burial of enormous quantities of small serpentine
blocks; a deep square or rectangular pit was dug and filled up
by layer upon layer of pavement composed of these greenish
stones, and in three cases a mosaic mask, believed to represent
a stylized jaguar, made of serpentine blocks with the openings
filled with coloured sands, was laid on top (*Ill. 1*). Almost

2 Altar 5, La Venta, Tabasco, showing adults with typical Olmec
faces holding baby were-jaguars with cleft heads

3 Colossal stone head with typical Olmec features, from La Venta.
Now at Villahermosa, Tabasco

immediately this was buried and hidden from sight until the archaeologists found it over 2,000 years later. One such offering, for such they must have been, contained some 1,200 tons of serpentine, and the total weight of it found on the site was estimated to be about 5,000 tons. Its source was 112 miles away as the crow flies and some 350 miles by water. Similarly, the basaltic columns used on the site were brought 240 miles. Other things found were four colossal basalt heads with loose-lipped puffy faces, the largest over 8 feet high *(Ill. 3)*, also several stelae and massive basalt blocks, generally called altars *(Ill. 2)*, bearing carved figures

4 Offering 4, La Venta. Sixteen Olmec figurines and six celts forming a ceremonial group. The jade celts make a background, and one figurine, of conglomerate, leans against them. The other figurines are of serpentine or jade

and groups in high or low relief, many of them with similar loose-lipped 'baby faces'. Similar heads from San Lorenzo, another Olmec site, show signs of having been coated with plaster and painted. There were also caches which include jade and serpentine celts, also figurines representing curious sexless individuals with baby faces like those on the large monuments. The most remarkable of these consisted of sixteen figurines grouped in front of a row of six slender jade celts as though taking part in a ceremony *(Ill. 4)*. Study of Olmec art from this and other centres has shown that there is a series grading from baby faces at one end to jaguar ones at the other, and a mutilated carving at Potrero Nuevo, another Olmec site, which appears to show a jaguar copulating with a woman, has suggested that the baby-faced or jaguar-faced monstrosities were thought to be the result of such a union. They have been given the name of were-jaguars. Many of them are shown with notched or cleft skulls, and it may be that certain infants having this deformity were regarded as examples *(Ill. 5)*. On some carvings they are shown as squalling babies *(Ill. 6)* and on others they are elaborately dressed and float in the air holding clubs. It has been shown that the faces may have developed into those of the rain gods in later cultures, hence it is thought that the were-jaguars may have been celestial rain spirits. Some stelae and other monuments bear carvings in low relief showing richly adorned personages with aquiline noses wearing elaborate head-dresses, which may have a sort of chin-strap *(Ill. 7)*. In some cases they seem to be bearded, and all have such strong individuality that they are thought to be portraits. They may be accompanied by baby-faced dwarfs, as on a stela from Alvarado, Veracruz, and possibly on some of the La Venta monuments, which shows that they are contemporary and part of the same Olmec heritage. One example appears on Monument 19 at La Venta in the curve of a serpent, who may

5 Jade celt representing an Olmec figure, combining delicate engraving ▶
with heavy carving. The eyebrow fringes are very characteristic

well be the forerunner of the plumed serpent god, Quetzalcóatl, who has such a prominent place in the religion and art of Classic and Post-Classic times *(Ill. 7)*.

La Venta was a remote island site, far from the maize patches of the peasants who supported it, and this may have been a reason for choosing it as a holy place. It is believed that its resident population could not have been more than about 150, composed of the priestly ruling class, their attendants and master craftsmen. For their support and the building work of the sanctuary, it is thought that there would have been a widely scattered population of some 18,000 people. It would be difficult to exaggerate the strength of the drive, and of the control exercised by a few men over a multitude, which caused these enormous structures to be erected, these vast quantities of stone to be carried so far, and so much time, energy and skill to be expended on these great carvings, all for non-material ends. La Venta, which could in many aspects be regarded as a typically Classic site, seems to have been abandoned and many of its monuments defaced about 400 B C, several centuries before the Classic Period proper began.

6   Reclining infantile Olmec figurine

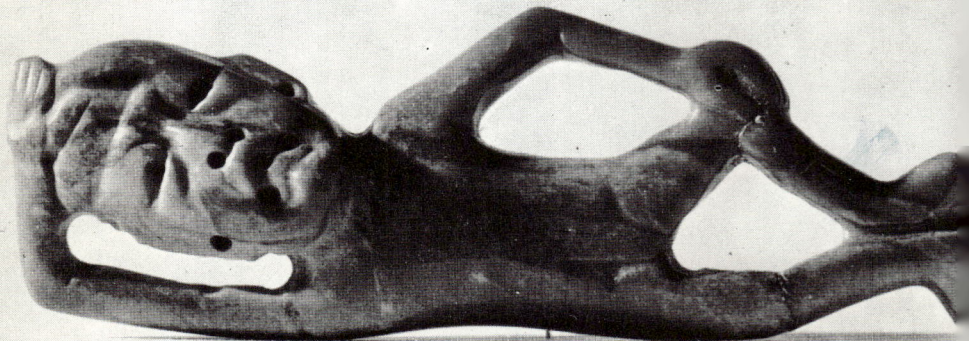

7 Monument 19, from La Venta, showing figure with jaguar head-
dress overshadowed by a plumed rattlesnake. Now at Villahermosa

Olmec art is essentially naturalistic and not abstract, in spite of the mythical character of the were-jaguar which is the most frequent subject depicted in some form or other. The abstract character of the jaguar mask mosaics at La Venta is a rare exception, although faces engraved on jades are occasionally shown similarly by means of a vertical bar for the nose, a pair of circles for the eyes and another pair of circles for the mouth. The V-shaped depression in the top of the head links these masks with the more usual were-jaguar baby with its cleft head. In contrast, the famous bearded wrestler now known to come from the hamlet of Antonio Plaza on the Uxpanapa river in southern Veracruz is a splendid realistic example which may well be a portrait of an actual person *(Ill. 9)*. Olmec objects, celts, masks and even figurines, generally have rectangular or trapezoidal outlines with rounded corners and slightly convex sides, which gives an effect of massiveness and strength even to the smallest examples, an effect which is shared alike by the gigantic heads and the small jade figurines *(Ill. 8)*.

9 Basalt Olmec figure of a realistic type, known as 'The Wrestler,' from Antonio Plaza, Veracruz

A frequent feature is a combination of carving in relief and very delicate engraving on a single object, particularly on the masks, figurines and celts of the dark grey-green jade which is so characteristic of the style. Reliefs on stelae fill the spaces they occupy in a satisfying manner like well-drawn heraldic charges, but they do not sprawl all over the background in the way that Maya designs do. The figures in reliefs are generally shown in profile with the feet pointing in the same direction, as in the early stages of Maya art.

The greatest concentration of Olmec remains is found in the limited tropical Gulf Coast area where La Venta lies, and this was doubtless the homeland of the art style, but signs of its presence are known from a far wider area. Rock carvings, which could not be transported and hence prove the presence of Olmec artists, are found as far away as Chalchuapa, El Salvador, where two figures, probably warriors, have typical Olmec profiles and were-jaguar faces. A masked figure at San Isidro Piedra Parada, Guatemala, is more akin to the presumed portrait reliefs of the home area on the Gulf Coast. Nearer home, there are examples at Chalcatcingo, Morelos, which include a group of three elaborately helmeted warriors brandishing war clubs, two of whom wear bird masks and threaten a naked bearded prisoner. These again relate rather to the portrait reliefs of La Venta than to the were-jaguars, and like the other two examples they have been thought to show that the Olmec presence in the outlying areas consisted of invading warriors.

More frequent and widespread are small portable objects such as jade figurines, and plaques and celts with incised designs. Many are unprovenanced, but a number come from Puebla, Morelos and the Valley of Mexico, with a notable concentration in Guerrero. This suggested to Covarrubias, the noted Mexican artist and one of the pioneers in Olmec studies, that Guerrero was the original Olmec homeland, but the knowledge now available about the Gulf Coast area has shown that this view cannot reasonably be sustained. From Guerrero comes the one surviving wooden Olmec object, a mask encrusted with pieces of jade *(Ill. 10)*. The

10 The only surviving wooden Olmec object, a mask inlaid with jade from Cañon de la Mano, Iguala, Guerrero

11 White-slipped hollow Olmec pottery figurine from Tlatilco, on the outskirts of Mexico City

Valley of Mexico seems to be the northern limit of the style, but portable Olmec objects are found thinly scattered far to the south, the remotest being two jade figurines with bat-like wings from Costa Rica.

Two hollow pottery figurines which, from their fragility, suggest local manufacture, were found at Gualupita, Morelos, but the most remarkable example of Olmec influence is at Tlatilco, a Formative Period village of unique character near Mexico City. Among many objects of local types, a small proportion of distinctively Olmec pottery figurines have been found *(Ill. 11)*, as well as a few jade ones, and Olmec influence is also seen in the jaguar claws which are engraved on some pottery vessels.

12 Two columns of carved glyphs, Monte Albán I. Monte Albán, Oaxaca. They have not been read, but must, from later analogies, be calendrical

13 *Danzante* with glyph near the mouth. Monte Albán I. Monte Albán, Oaxaca

The effects of Olmec influence were not confined to the spread of carvings and portable objects in pure Olmec style, and other signs of it in the shape of Olmec-derived styles can be detected both in its own time span and later. The first of these is exemplified in Oaxaca by the Monte Albán I stage, beginning about 700 B C. Within the great Zapotec centre of Monte Albán (*Ill. 74*) can be seen a number of stone slabs bearing incised figures of naked men, probably corpses, in loose-limbed, floppy, tumbling postures, called *Los Danzantes* (The Dancers), which were set in a stone-faced platform hidden under later buildings (*Ill. 13*). They lack many specifically Olmec features, but the mouths of some are Olmec in character and the overall effect points strongly to Olmec influence. Unlike true Olmec monuments they are accompanied by definite glyphs, carved on the figures themselves and on separate slabs *(Ill. 12)*. Monte Albán I pottery, found at Monte Albán itself and the neighbouring site of Monte Negro, includes incense burners which are decorated with strongly Olmecoid faces *(Ill. 14)* and pots with narrow spouts at the side, a type which survived into later periods. Like most of the later Zapotec pottery in the same area, it is a monochrome grey ware.

14 Face urn of grey pottery, with Olmecoid mouth. Monte Albán I. Monte Negro, Oaxaca

15 Grey pottery jar, Monte Albán I, from Nochistlán, Oaxaca. This type, with lateral spout, carries over into the subsequent stage

Tres Zapotes is a site some 100 miles north-west of La Venta which has given plenty of evidence of occupation during the period when the latter flourished, including a colossal basalt head, but it continued after La Venta's destruction. To the later stage belongs Stela C, a slab bearing a date which, in the Maya bar-and-dot system, corresponds to 31 B C. This is earlier than any known Maya inscription, and if the systems are the same, as they surely must be, it is the earliest dated monument in the New World. On the other side of it is a highly stylized were-jaguar type of face, showing Olmec inspiration but not itself Olmec.

There are many other monuments at Tres Zapotes, but they point more forward to the Classic Period than backward to the Olmec. They belong to a style which is found also on a stela at

El Mesón, central Veracruz, as well on a number of monuments far away on the tropical Pacific coastal plain at Izapa, Chiapas, near the Guatemalan border, at Kaminaljuyú on the outskirts of Guatemala City, and at other places. The style has been named Izapa, but this does not imply that it necessarily originated there and it may well have started on the Gulf Coast. Thorough studies of Izapa, is which a large and important site, have not yet been published, but it is known that the monuments are placed within groups of courts like those normally found in Mesoamerican ceremonial centres and that the earthen mounds surrounding the courts are in some cases faced with cobble stones. Stelae bearing figures and complex groups are found at these sites *(Ill. 16)*, and like the later Maya ones many of them are accompanied by an 'altar' which may, in their case, take the form of a giant toad, a rain symbol *(Ill. 17)*. Human figures and gods are shown with the legs in profile as though walking, but with the body partly turned towards the viewer and the head again in profile like early Maya ones. The chief god has a trunk-like upper lip, apparently an exaggeration of the loose lip of the Olmec were-jaguar, and is a forerunner of the long-nosed Maya rain god. In contrast with the Olmec style, scrolls and appendages begin to sprawl over backgrounds in the manner adopted by the Maya. Monument C at Tres Zapotes shows armed figures floating in the air, and these are thought to be a florid version of the sort of scene shown on some Olmec carvings, such as Stela 3 at La Venta. At El Baúl, Guatemala, there is a stela carved in the Izapa style which bears a date corresponding to A D 36, a little later than the Tres Zapotes date already referred to, on the assumption, which is entirely reasonable, that they are both written in the system normally associated with the Maya at a later date. Covarrubias suggested long ago that the monuments of the Izapa style were permeated in general by the Olmec spirit, but in many other respects it is not difficult to see features in common with early Maya work. The Izapa style is regarded, with reason, as a connecting link in time and space between the Olmec civilization and the Classic Maya which came after.

16 Stela 5, Izapa, Chiapas, showing a complex scene

17 Stela 3, with toadlike Altar 2 at Izapa. The stela is one of a group which ▶
are framed above and below but not at the sides. It appears to depict
a figure accompanied by a feathered serpent

28

THE VALLEY OF MEXICO: *Formative and Classic*

The figurines which were the first feelers towards art at the villages round the great lake have already been mentioned, and so have the Olmec influences at Tlatilco. This was an exceptional place in other respects also, and in an attempt to explain the differences between it and its neighbours it has been described as an aristocratic village in the midst of ones of lower class. Olmec influences have also been held responsible for the differences, but Olmec objects amount to only a small minority of the material, and there may also have been influences from some other direction, at present unknown. The chief differences were the greater richness of the burials and the presence of special types of pottery and figurines. Brown, black, red and white pottery is found, with a limited amount of painted decoration in red and white or yellow *(Ill. 22)*, and there are many forms of bowl and jar, but the outstanding examples are vessels modelled to represent fish, birds, animals and gourds in a very accomplished manner, the best being in polished black ware *(Ills. 20, 21)*. Among the

18 *(far left)* Head of a pottery figurine from the Valley of Mexico

19 *(above left)* Female figurine of the Formative Period, Valley of Mexico, modelled in a non-Tlatilco style

20, 21 *(right)* Two polished black-ware vessels representing a fish and a dog. Part of the fish bowl has an unpolished surface, originally tinted red with haematite. Tlatilco

22 Bowl showing diamonds and stripes in brown to brownish grey, the colour of the ware, against a ground of red to dark red paint, the variations being due to firing differences. The designs are outlined by incision. Tlatilco

peculiar forms is a bottle with a spout in the shape of a stirrup, in which two branches rise from the top of the closed vessel and join to form a single tubular opening above. This type becomes most common in Peru at a later date, and there is reason to believe that it was one of several elements carried there from Mexico early in the first millennium B C. One remarkable vessel has the form of a rapidly tapering screw. The chief forms of surface decoration are produced by roughening or otherwise differentiating certain zones, which are limited by broad incised lines, and several processes are used. The zones may simply be left unpolished, or they may be recessed by scraping, or covered with stabbed dots or with rocker stamping, a series of zig-zag lines produced by rocking a curved object like the edge of a mollusc shell over the surface. Recessed areas may be tinted red by rubbing in haematite powder after firing. These processes are used to depict hands, jaguar claws and snakes, as well as geometrical forms.

32

23, 24 Male figurine wearing helmet and two-headed female pottery figurine with traces of black painting on yellow. Both from Tlatilco

Also of pottery are remarkable figurines *(Ills. 23, 24)*, which are much superior to those of the neighbouring sites *(Ills. 18, 19)*. Many are of women, young or old, naked or wearing a short skirt, and some are painted with lines and patches in black, red and yellow, perhaps applied in life with pottery roller stamps, of which many have been found here. Many are very graceful, some have rattles on the legs and appear to be dancing, some hold a child, and one is playing with a dog. Some have two heads, and some a Siamese twin double head, in which each is complete apart from sharing a central eye. There are men with masks, probably shamans, and others with helmets, also hunchbacks, dwarfs, acrobats, musicians playing drums, and even the first known player of the ball-game, which was played right up to the Spanish conquest, shown with protection on right hand, knee and ankle, but otherwise wearing only a loin-cloth. There are pottery masks, showing human or animal faces, natural or grotesque, the most remarkable of which is divided vertically into half a face with protruding

33

25 Pottery mask, half face with protruding tongue, and half skull. Tlatilco

tongue and half a skull, presumably symbolizing life and death
(*Ill. 25*). Dualism of this kind is found also in Chavín culture
masks of much the same age in Peru, whither it is thought to
have travelled with other things from Mexico. Tlatilco is thought
to have been first settled about 800 B C.

After Tlatilco there were no artistic developments of any importance in the Valley before the beginning of the Classic Period.
That the idea of the ceremonial centre was present there in late
Formative times, the last three centuries B C and the first two or
three A D, is shown by the massive tiered conical platform at
Cuicuilco on the outskirts of Mexico City. This differs from most
later pyramids in having a round rather than a square or rectangular plan, and in having two great ramps rather than stairways
for its ascent. It was built of layers of clay and rubble faced
with volcanic rock, and it seems to have been raised in stages.
It supported successively three superimposed elliptical clay altars
covered with a coating of brilliant red cinnabar.

The last century B C saw the rise of Teotihuacán some 30 miles
to the north-east, but it was not until the second stage here

34

26 Earlier stage of the main pyramid in the Ciudadela at Teotihuacán, showing feathered serpents with rattlesnake tails and rain god masks. Note also the sea shells indicating contact with the coast

that the Classic Period really began. This great centre, in size and influence probably the most important of all Classic sites, is grouped about a great avenue running at least two miles on a line 17 degrees east of north. At its north end is a great stone-faced pyramid now called the Pyramid of the Moon and near by and to the east of the avenue is a greater one called the Pyramid of the Sun, facing at right angles to the avenue towards the sunset on the day the sun is at its zenith. It was sadly mutilated by injudicious restoration many years ago. On either side of the avenue are the remains of smaller pyramids, platforms, courts and palaces, few of which have been excavated and restored although work on them is now proceeding actively and scientifically. The grouping is orderly but does not attempt to be symmetrical. Unlike most Classic centres Teotihuacán was a city, that is to say the ceremonial nucleus was surrounded by the dwellings of the people, a development which was not possible in the forests in which the great Maya centres were built, and in other cases was prevented by the topography.

Religious architecture at Teotihuacán is based on the principle of the slope and panel, that is to say the pyramids and platforms, made of adobe (mud brick) with stone facings, are composed of steps, each of which consists of a recessed vertical panel with a plain frame of rectangular section, standing on a much lower slope, which is overshadowed by the frame of the panel (*Ill. 27*). In the court known as the Ciudadela the chief pyramid shows an earlier stage in which the panels are filled with monumental sculpture, showing feathered rattlesnakes which meander along them with their heads alternating with the stylized bespectacled faces of the rain god (*Ill. 26*). Sea shells accompany the serpents' bodies, and serpents also adorn the supporting slopes and the balustrades of the great stairway. Like so many Mesoamerican monuments, this was hidden by a later and larger pyramid, whose slopes and panels are plain though they may at one time have been plastered and painted.

The 'palace' groups, thought to have been the residences of the élite, are arranged round rectangular courts. They have open

27 Main pyramid in the Ciudadela at Teotihuacán which illustrates a slope-and-panel profile. The earlier stage is seen in the background

fronts, with the roofs supported by square or rectangular columns, which may be carved with stiff figures in low relief. They are crowned with battlement-like crestings, in which the merlons may bear motifs such as the mouth of the rain god.

Apart from the carvings already mentioned, little monumental sculpture attributable to Teotihuacán has survived. The chief example is the great basalt figure, said to be a water goddess, which looks like a support for an architectural feature. Its outline is squat and is built up chiefly of squares and rectangles, and even the face is almost rectangular, although it tapers very slightly downwards. The figure is clothed in the skirt and *huipil*, a sort of blouse, which are still widely used by Mexican women, and there are large circular ear ornaments. The head supports a rectangular block. It is typical of the severe rectilinear character of high-

37

28   Stone mask of Teotihuacán style, found at Cholula

land Classic sculpture.   A somewhat similar statue, from Coatlichán,
near Texcoco, now stands outside the National Museum of Anthropology in Mexico City.   On a small scale, the same style is exemplified by the alabaster ocelot-bowl in the British Museum, and by
a jaguar from recent excavations at Teotihuacán *(Ill. 29)*.   Of the
other small sculptures, the most characteristic are the stone masks
(Ill. 28), at least some of which could have been used as false
faces for mummy bundles.   They are softer in outline than the
giant figures and the animals, but the widely-set oval eyes, the
straight or gently curved top, and the delicately-shaped slightly
open mouth give a highly characteristic appearance of great serenity.
The eyes are recessed, apparently to receive a coloured inlay, and
it has been suggested that the form of the top was intended to fit
under a head-dress of soft materials.

29 Jaguar of alabaster found during the recent work at Teotihuacán. A somewhat similar object, a bowl said to represent an ocelot, is in the British Museum

Chronological stages at Teotihuacán are marked by different styles of figurine (*Ill. 31*). The earliest, which precede the building of the great pyramids, share some characteristics with those of the simpler villages by the lake. They have markedly prognathous faces, and the mouths and eyes are formed by applied strips of clay. In both first and second stages broad headgear is similarly shown, and the rare complete ones are dressed in capes and skirts in some cases. In the second period, when the pyramids were being built, the figurines were more delicately modelled, there is less prognathism, the nose is deftly pinched out to a fine point, and the eyes and mouth formed by cuts. It has been suggested that the rectilinear style of sculpture belongs to this stage. In the third stage modelling is much more accomplished, and the faces resemble those of the stone masks. Some examples were made in moulds. They are sometimes described as the portrait type, with little justification since their outstanding feature is standardization. They generally wear only a loin-cloth, and some already have articulated arms and legs, originally attached to the trunk by cords. A few gods accompany the human figures, notably the fire god with his wrinkled face. In both stages two and three there may be a depression or notch in the top of the head, which may be an inheritance from the cleavage of the heads of the Olmec were-jaguar babies. Stage four is marked by a great outburst of decorative detail and a great variety of types, which accompany the invariable use of moulds. Most are elaborately dressed, with accessories like great feathered head-dresses, and some are stylized into squat conical shapes. The ringed eyes of the rain god are of frequent occurrence (*Ill. 30*), and it is probable that most of the figures depict gods of some kind, in contrast with the predominance of human beings at earlier stages. This stage is believed to date from after the destruction of Teotihuacán, which took place about A D 600 according to recent studies, and most of the figurines belonging to it come from Atzcapotzalco and other sites where the civilization lingered on.

Pottery shapes are highly characteristic, particularly a flat-based tripod with straight or slightly concave sides, vertical or

30 Pottery stamp showing head of rain god
with elaborate head-dress in relief.

31   Series of figurine heads : *a* first stage; *b* second stage ;
c-d third stage; *e* fourth stage Teotihuacán

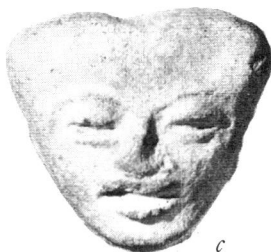

sloping gently outwards, and small nubbin feet, made in brown ware *(Ill. 32)*. Some such tripods have cylindrical or slab-shaped feet, which may be hollow. They may have incised designs, or part of the surface may be cut away and rubbed with red haematite, forming champlevé decoration, and the finest are covered with stucco, with mythological designs, gods or priests, formed by inlaying patches of different colours, red, blue-green, black, yellow and white *(Ill. 33)*. This decoration, which is generally called paint cloisonné, cannot by any stretch of the imagination be called a potter's technique, and is very fragile so that few examples have survived intact, but the effect is gorgeous indeed. Some vessels of this shape have a conical, fitting lid with a knob at the top, which may take the form of a head, often that of a bird. Other forms include flat-based jars with a globular or high-shouldered body surmounted by a flaring neck. A variety of this, called a *florero* or flower vase, has a small body and a trumpet-shaped neck of exaggerated height, flaring out to a diameter greater than that of the body *(Ill. 34)*. This type, like several others, is generally made in grey ware.

33 Jar covered with polychrome stucco, the decoration including a rain god face with elaborate headdress. Teotihuacán

32, 34 Two tripod vessels in brown ware with nubbin feet. Teotihuacán. One *(far left)* has applied mask and negatively painted brown dots on black, the other *(left)* has simple decoration made by burnishing part of the surface

An art which was extensively practised at Teotihuacán was mural painting, probably in true fresco, of which some of the most striking examples have been found in outlying 'palace' groups, probably the dwellings of the élite ; some have perished since their discovery but are known from copies. Alongside the avenue is a buried platform, known from its position to be early in date, which has the panels painted with interlaced scrolls, related to Classic carvings of the Gulf Coast, with green roundels on a red ground on the frames. Similarly simple paintings are to be seen on the so-called Temple of the Quetzal Bird-Butterfly, discovered recently near the Pyramid of the Moon. Here the rooms have delicate frets and step designs in white on a rose-red ground, framed by a line from which a row of hooks projects inwards, all in white. Part of the red ground is powdered with dark discs originally of shining brown mica. Among many figure designs, also near the nucleus of the site, are an elaborately dressed warrior in profile with shield and blunt arrows, and a sun disc on an altar flanked by even more richly-dressed priests. Priests and warrior have what must be speech scrolls emerging from the mouth, although they do not bear anything resembling a glyph. A painting which has perished shows a scene in which stiffly-drawn seated or standing figures in profile make offerings to a pair of massive statues recalling the great stone water goddess, before which stand great spider-like pyres. The whole rests on a wavy base representing water. At Atetelco, an outlying group, are jaguars and coyotes in profile, framed by an interlacing border made up of parts of the same animals. At another outlying site, Tetitla, is a pair of stiff, squat full-face rain gods, with vast plumed head-dresses bearing an owl-like rain god mask *(Ill. 35)*, within a frame of interlaced serpents. In the same group is a striking painting, part of which has been removed and is now in the Bliss collection in the United States. It shows a priest disguised as a jaguar, wearing an enormous plume of feathers on his head and carrying a shield and a plumed sceptre-like rattle, approaching a temple along a path marked by footprints. He wears a net costume on which his disguise is mounted, a characteristic of the priests of the Aztec

35 Wall painting, Tetitla, Teotihuacán. Rain god with blue scrolls representing water, and other objects, flowing from his hands

rain god Tlaloc in later times, and the background consists of thin cusped diagonal bands of blue-grey and green on a rose-red ground, from which depend deep fringes composed of long thin triangles of darker red, which has been interpreted as a rain symbol. This painting as a whole is in two shades of red, green, blue-grey and yellow, a very usual Teotihuacán combination, to which black and white may be added and bright blue take the place of the blue-grey. Throughout the whole series there is a predominant interest in water and the rain god *(Ill. 36)*, which may betray a growing shortage as the population increased and more woods were cut down to supply fuel to burn lime for the vast amount of plaster needed in the buildings. The same interest is shown in a painting at Tepantitla, another of the outlying groups, in a style

45

36 Wall painting recently discovered at Teotihuacán showing rain god sowing, with speech scrolls emerging from his mouth

which contrasts with the static character of the others and must surely be the latest in the series *(Ill. 37)*. It shows lively little human figures with speech scrolls, dressed only in loin-cloths, dancing, swimming, chasing butterflies and monkeys, waving branches, picking flowers or resting, in well-watered tropical surroundings, done in blue, green, yellow and pink on the usual dark red ground. Above it are the remains of a rain god, exceptionally florid even for Teotihuacán, standing on bands of complex scrolls denoting water, in which are starfish and peculiar swimming creatures. Drops fall from his hands, and priests attend him on either side. The scene is thought to represent the rain god's paradise, where the souls of those who please him are in bliss.

About A D 600 Teotihuacán was destroyed, but as I have said the culture lingered on elsewhere. During the next two centuries some of the people returned to the ruins as treasure hunters, and a great pit in the court of the Temple of the Quetzal Bird-Butterfly testifies to their activities. That they were related to the original users of the site is demonstrated by the potsherds they left behind.

37 *(opposite)* Partly reconstructed wall painting, Tepantitla, Teotihuacán, showing figures disporting themselves in the rain god's paradise, over which he presides. He is separated from the scene below by a band of interlacing serpents, among which is a small rain god ▶

The great Classic centres of Mesoamerica are thought to have been ruled by a priestly class. Their most important buildings were religious, and they have no signs of fortifications, indeed most of them were sited in places incapable of defence. There are no indications of any but local fighting, and no evidence for a ruling warrior class. The centres had widespread contacts with one another and influenced each other, but did not build empires. Although it came to an end some three centuries before most of the others, Teotihuacán was in its prime extremely influential, and may well have been the most influential of them all. Signs of its contacts with the Gulf Coast can be seen in some of the figurines and other pottery of Remojadas in Veracruz, and Gulf Coast scrolls can be seen on Teotihuacán pottery as well as on the mural already cited. Many of the best stone masks of Teotihuacán style come from Guerrero. Much further away, at Kaminaljuyú, on the outskirts of Guatemala City, is a pyramid which shares many specific features with the Pyramid of the Moon, and there are many nearly cylindrical covered tripod pots of pure Teotihuacán shape, decorated with Maya designs in the Teotihuacán 'paint cloisonné' stucco technique. In this case the relationships are so intimate that they can reasonably be explained only by the presence of artificers from Teotihuacán, and probably of those who directed them. Besides widespread evidence of trading contacts in the intermediate areas, such as Teotihuacán pottery on Maya sites and Maya jades in Teotihuacán, there is increasing evidence for the sharing of ideas, such as is shown by the recent discovery of a rain god of Teotihuacán form and style carved on a slab at the great Maya site of Tikal. Some more general resemblances, such as that of the faces on the Classic Zapotec funerary urns of Monte Albán to the stone masks of Teotihuacán, and features like the wide distribution of forbears of the later Mixtec year sign, a rectangle interlaced with an inverted V, in Teotihuacán, Oaxaca and Maya sites, may point to a common cultural ancestor, perhaps in the Olmec civilization.

Teotihuacán is the best known of the highland Classic sites of central Mexico, but it is not the only one. An early building period in the great pyramid at Cholula in Puebla for example, shows the use of the slope and panel in much the same form as that of Teotihuacán. Cholula has had a very long occupation, from late Formative times until the present, when a Colonial church crowns a considerable hill, the weathered remains of the largest pyramid in the Americas.

THE VALLEY OF MEXICO: *Post-Classic*

The fall of Teotihuacán marked the beginning of a period of obscurity, which probably reflects a real confusion in the affairs of the Valley of Mexico. Paradoxically, the surviving documents, the oldest of which were written in late pre-Conquest times, reach back at the earliest to about this period. To the south arose the sanctuary of Xochicalco in Morelos, a hill-top site of complex plan culminating in an ornate platform crowned by a temple, both of slope-and-panel outline. This differs from the Teotihuacán type in that the slope is much higher than the panel, which is crowned by an overhanging chamfered cornice. This reduces the strong horizontal emphasis given by the heavily-framed panels of Teotihuacán, and gives a larger field for sculpture on the amplified slope. There is a facing of carved andesite slabs, having wavy feathered serpents on the lower slope with glyphs and seated dignitaries in the waves, and similar seated figures and glyphs in the panels and on the slope of the temple wall. The decoration shows strong Maya influence, and there is a ball-court elsewhere on the site with the sloping walls found at some Classic Maya centres like Copán and Piedras Negras. This is the earliest known ball-court in Central Mexico. The main buildings at Xochicalco are believed to date from late Classic times and to have continued in occupation into the Post-Classic, which in Mesoamerica was marked by the rise of a ruling military class and the increasing prominence of warfare and human sacrifice. Xochicalco, standing on its terraced hill-top, was fortified with walls and moats, and some of the figures carved on its platform have been identified as warriors. Its civilization is thought to have been one of the strands from which the subsequent Toltec one was spun.

The Toltecs exemplify the early Post-Classic Period in central Mexico. They seem to have been a mixture of peoples from various sources, the chief of whom were originally barbarians from the north-west, but more civilized elements from the Gulf Coast, Puebla and Xochicalco also played their part. Their most important remains are at Tula, Hidalgo, some 40 miles north-west of Mexico City, which was their capital, at any rate in their heyday from about the mid-tenth century to the mid-twelfth (A D 968—1168 in the opinion of some historians, but some would prolong it into the thirteenth century). Along with the settled agricultural life, the barbarians quickly adopted many of the features of the civilization of their predecessors and associates, including imposing ceremonial buildings. The rapidity with which the civilizing process occurred calls for a brief remark, since the same happened to subsequent barbarian immigrants from the same quarter. Many of the original inhabitants of the Valley must still have lived there, and doubtless greatly outnumbered their conquerors, who can for their part have had little in the way of a cultural and artistic heritage of their own. It would therefore be natural to expect the newcomers to absorb much of what they found, though they might well make profound changes in its content. The great change to be seen at Tula is an abundance of signs of a preoccupation with war, and it came to a violent end. After its overthrow it was so thoroughly destroyed that few believed that it could have been the Toltec capital, until excavation revealed its size.

The pyramid which has been most fully studied is faced with stone, and over this was laid an outer facing of carved slabs secured by tenons. It has five stages, with yet another variety of the old slope-and-panel facing, a lower plain slope and a 'panel' divided into two, the upper division being roughly equal in height to the slope and the lower slightly greater. The upper division has a row of passant jaguars and coyotes framed above and below with a plain square moulding, and the lower has pairs of eagles eating human hearts, similarly framed, with a recessed panel between each pair bearing a composite crouching monster crowned with feathers, which is identified as the feathered serpent god

50

38 Tula. Remains of facing on east side of north pyramid, showing two sets of friezes of jaguars, coyotes, eagles and monsters

called by the Aztecs Quetzalcóatl, in the guise of the morning star *(Ill. 38)*. The whole was formerly plastered and painted. The jaguars and eagles are thought to be the insignia of orders of warriors, the predecessors of the well-known Aztec orders, but the arrangement of the jaguars also resembles the older painted frieze at Atetelco, Teotihuacán. The pyramid was crowned by a temple of which little remains but four great standing figures, 15 feet high *(Ill. 39)*, and four square piers bearing carving in low relief, which must have supported the roof. Each consists of four separate stones tenoned together, which had been thrown down and scattered. The figures are grim warriors carrying spears and spear-throwers, and every detail of their dress and insignia is carefully carved on their massive columnar bodies, down to the knots which tie their garters. Several features connect them with the feathered serpent. The piers are covered with rather

39 Tula. Warri figure and tv square columns basalt. Top north pyramid

40 Tula. North pyramid with remains of vestibule and colonnade below

stiff, wiry carvings representing Toltec warriors in rather a shamb-
ling attitude, with legs and head in profile and body in three-
quarter view like the much older early Classic Maya figures, alternating with bundles of arrows. Generally, the style of carving
recalls that on the composite piers in the Temple of the Quetzal
Bird-Butterfly at Teotihuacán. A new feature here is a large
vestibule at the foot of the pyramid stairway *(Ill. 40)*, which had
three rows of square piers supporting the roof. Behind the
pyramid is a wall about 8 feet 6 inches high called the serpent
wall, carved with rattlesnakes eating human skeletons and crowned
with a cresting of scrolls inspired by sections of conch shells, a
symbol of Quetzalcóatl. Gone are the lively little figures of the
rain god's paradise at Teotihuacán, gone is the exaggerated floridity
of the later paintings of the god himself, everywhere are signs of
that obsession with war and death which was to reach such a
climax in Aztec times.

The god who is most prominent in the art of Tula is the feathered
serpent, Quetzalcóatl, and at that site at least the rain god suffers
something of an eclipse. Confusion has been caused by the adoption

53

of the name by the ruler who founded the city, called in full Ce Acatl Topiltzin Quetzalcóatl (Ce Acatl, One Reed, being the day of his birth), around whom many legends have gathered, some concerning the god and some the prince. He is described as being at enmity with a more warlike god, Tezcatlipoca, the smoking mirror, named from an obsidian or haematite mirror which replaces his right foot, and it appears that shortly before A D 1000 a rival faction of this god's devotees expelled Quetzalcóatl and his followers. They wandered away to the south-east and disappeared overseas, prophesying their return, a story which had its consequences when Montezuma thought that Cortés and his followers were they. It is more than a coincidence that carvings virtually identical with those at Tula appeared on a whole series of new buildings dating from the end of the first millennium at the old Maya site of Chichén Itzá in Yucatán, and that a Mexican ruler named Kukulcán, meaning feathered serpent in Maya, is reputed in Maya legend to have appeared there in A D 987. At Tula itself, it is curious that there are many carvings alluding to Quetzalcóatl but none to Tezcatlipoca.

41 Toltec Mazápan ware bowl, painted in orange on buff with groups of wavy lines

Apart from the carvings at Tula, many of which have been mentioned, little remains of Toltec art, apart from some characteristic pottery styles. The chief of these, of local manufacture, is Mazápan ware (*Ill. 41*), orange to buff in colour, generally in the form of bowls which are decorated inside with groups of parallel wavy lines painted with a composite brush. Less important is a red-on-cream ware named Matlatzinca (*Ill. 43*). A trade ware which had a wide distribution at this time was Plumbate (*Ill. 42*), named from its appearance but not its composition, which is ascribed to the west coast near the Guatemalan frontier. Sherds of it are found in the Toltec refuse at Tula. It takes many forms, some of them human or animal effigy vessels, and is grey or brown in colour. It is extremely hard, has a vitreous lustre, and is properly described as a glazed ware. Glazing is almost unknown in ancient America, except in parts of the south-west of the U.S.A. where a dark lead glaze paint may be used for linear decoration but not for covering a surface. In the case of Plumbate ware, there is no lead in the glaze, which is thought to owe its existence to the physical properties of the clay. Pottery figurines continued to be made in moulds at this time, but there is nothing remarkable about them.

The end of Tula was brought about by the arrival of further waves of nomads from the north-west, called collectively the Chichimecs, who do not appear to have differed materially from the nomadic component of the Toltecs. They belonged to various tribes which, with one exception, had a common language, Nahuatl, and as they settled down and acquired some of the features of the civilization of the surviving Toltecs and other inhabitants of the Valley, they set up a number of small states which were constantly fighting among themselves. One group settled in 1224 at Tenayuca, a short distance to the north of Mexico City. Here they rebuilt a pyramid first constructed in Toltec times, which has been carefully excavated to show the eight reconstructions that it has undergone. It carried twin temples on the top, like the great pyramid at Tenochtitlán, the Aztec capital where Mexico City now stands, and it was surrounded by a ring of stone snakes, whose carved heads and tails were united by a body made of small stones in a matrix of lime

42 *(opposite)* Plumbate ware pot in form of animal with inlaid shell eyes. Trade ware of Toltec age

43 *(above)* Toltec Matlatzinca ware tripod bowl

mortar. They were originally plastered and painted, some green with black scales, and some with red bellies and black backs marked with white circles.

The Chichimecs of Tenayuca were followed by several other tribes, Acolhuas, Tepanecs and Otomís, and there was a great deal of fighting between them, ending with the emergence of the Aztecs as the predominant group in the fifteenth century. This is not the place to say more of the history and social institutions of the Aztecs than is necessary to the understanding of their art. They were great warriors, probably the fiercest of all in Mexico. Their tribal god was Huitzilopochtli, a war god who came to be identified with the sun. He had an unquenchable thirst for human blood and especially for human hearts, to sustain him in his struggles with his jealous elder sister the moon, and brothers the stars, who were gods of the night, born before him of the earth goddess, Coatlicué. Each morning he had to overcome them, in order to rise and pursue his journey through the sky. Above all he needed the hearts of warriors taken in battle, and this accentuated the ferocity of the Aztec warriors. As the latest comers to a well-populated land they constantly had to be ejected from territories claimed by others, and this increased the unpopularity engendered by their barbarity. They eventually settled on an island adjoining the unpromising swampy land on the western shore of the great lake, and there founded Tenochtitlán about 1350. They thought of themselves as the chosen People of the Sun, destined to collaborate with the gods and, by feeding the sun, to prevent the world from coming to an end. They would be better able to do this and to obtain more prisoners if they dominated the other peoples of the world, and it was this more than anything which caused them to embark on their career of conquest in the fifteenth century. At the final dedication of the great temple at Tenochtitlán in 1488, with its twin shrines of Tlaloc, the rain god, and Huitzilopochtli, it is confidently stated that 20,000 prisoners were sacrificed by cutting out their hearts. It would have been remarkable enough if there had been only 200!

It is difficult to point to much that is indigenous in Aztec art, beyond a primitive brutality which is seen particularly in their

44 Jade showing extreme stylization of a sacrificial temple pyramid. Aztec

monumental sculpture, and which can easily be understood from what has already been said. Examples can be seen in the colossal statue of the earth goddess, Coatlicué, which was found in Mexico City on the site of the ceremonial centre of Tenochtitlán, and another from Coxcatlán, Puebla. The first is a block of nearly rectangular outline when seen from the front, with two fanged rattlesnake heads where the human head should be, a necklace of hearts and hands with a skull as the central ornament hanging over the pendant breasts, and a skirt of snakes *(Ill. 46)*. The other has a death's-head instead of the two snakes heads and lacks the necklace, but the grinning skull, the over-large raised hands and the serpent

45 Basalt mask showing the skin from face of a sacrificed victim as worn by priests of the god Xipe
46 *(opposite)* Colossal statue of the Aztec earth goddess Coatlicué ▶

skirt give an equally grim effect. In a more realistic but similarly horrific vein are some much smaller sculptures, such as the statuette showing a devotee or priest of Xipe, the flayed god, dressed in the skin of a sacrificed victim, and that showing a goddess giving birth, both in the Bliss Collection at Dumbarton Oaks. In the British Museum are the famous crystal skull and the stone Xipe masks (*Ill. 45*). These and many others, and the innumerable rattlesnakes of all sizes (*Ill. 49*), show a preoccupation with horror and death which is entirely in keeping with the character of the Aztecs.

47 The stone of Tizoc, with historical scenes influenced by Mixtec manuscripts

There were other strains in Aztec sculpture. One of them seems to show the influence of the painted manuscripts of the Mixtecs of Oaxaca, and among these a fine example is the great stone of Tizoc found in the centre of Tenochtitlán (*Ill. 47*). This is a low cylindrical drum, whose circumference bears scenes showing the conquests of Tizoc, fifth king of the Aztecs, who died in 1486. Few sculptures of this style have survived, and they are divided between historical scenes like those cited, and purely religious or mythological subjects like the well-known calendar stone from the same area. Another group consists of very attractive realistic carvings of animal or vegetable forms such as the giant red grasshopper, some 18 inches long (*Ill. 48*), the green stone pumpkin, and the basalt cactus, which were seen in Europe in the exhibition of Mexican art in 1952-53. These appear to be purely representational, but in view of the religious character of the equally naturalistic rattlesnakes, a similar religious function cannot be excluded.

62

48 Naturalistic red stone giant grasshopper,
with wings folded and legs drawn under the
body. Aztec

49 Miniature Aztec rattlesnake of black
stone veined with white, with a human head
between its jaws

The art of the Aztecs owes a great deal to what is called Mixteca-Puebla art, which belongs to the Mixtec people who lived mainly in Oaxaca, and especially to developments of it originating in the important and already ancient centre of Cholula in Puebla which must at this time have been within their sphere of influence. It is by no means devoid of brutality, for instance there are pictures of human sacrifice in the manuscripts; indeed this and many other features of Aztec religion, such as the gods Xipe, Quetzalcóatl and Tlaloc, had their origins far back in the past, but it is the exaggeration of barbarity which differentiates their religion and was reflected in their art.

The surviving Aztec wood-carvings are a few drums, gongs and spear-throwers, the latter embellished in some cases with gold leaf. They are all strongly under Mixtec influence and there is little to distinguish Mixtec from Aztec work, beyond an observation by Covarrubias that 'Mixtec *teponaztli* (horizontal cylindrical gongs) differ from the Aztec ones in that in the Mixtec gongs the sides are carved with small intricate designs in low relief *(Ill. 50)*, while Aztec ones tend to adapt the gong to the form of an animal or a human being' *(Ills. 51, 52)*. The great war drums, such as that from Malinalco, bear carvings which include eagles of the quality of the best medieval European heraldry.

50 Mixtec *teponaztli* (two-tongued drum), with intricate carved designs. Note the Mixtec year sign on bottom right-hand corner

51, 52 Two wooden Aztec (teponaztli). With owl carved on side (above) and in the form of a curly-haired animal (below)

65

53 (right) Aztec sacrificial knife, with chalcedony blade and wooden handle encrusted with malachite, turquoise and shell mosaic, representing an eagle warrior

54 (below) Head-dress given by Montezuma to Cortés as a gift for his sovereign. Mainly of green quetzal feathers, but blue, crimson, brown and white feathers were also used, as well as gold ornaments

Of jewellery and other minor works in metals and semi-precious
stones there is nothing to say, since all seem to have been brought
from Mixtec territory or made by Mixtec artists. Even the mosaic
objects in turquoise, red and white shell, pyrites and jet, such as
the handle of a sacrificial stone knife which represents an eagle
knight *(Ill. 53)*, and the mask whose base is the face of a human
skull, have both, along with others also in the British Museum,
been claimed as Mixtec work, but they are surely Aztec in spirit.
No pre-Conquest Aztec manuscript paintings have survived but
there are several which date from the first years after the Conquest
(e.g. Codices Borbonicus and Magliabecchi), as well as some
rather later ones when European influence had become fairly
strong (e.g. Codex Florentino). The first group includes calendrical matters, genealogies and tribute rolls, and comparisons with
surviving pre-Conquest Mixtec manuscripts suggest that their style
had changed very little. There are only rather minor differences
between them and the Mixtec ones, which will be mentioned
in their place. A minor art which can be considered a variety
of painting, or even of mosaic, is the feather work in which two

55 Orange tripod bowl with eagle in grey-black in the centre. Aztec III. Mexico City

layers of feathers, a lower one of medium-sized feathers and a top one of carefully selected small ones, were glued to a base of soft cloth. A few examples still exist, among them a round shield showing a blue coyote outlined with gold on a pink ground, said to be the name glyph of King Ahuizotl. Rather a different technique, in which the feathers were woven or sewn into the backing, was used for some objects, including Montezuma's magnificent tiara of green quetzal feathers *(Ill. 54)*. Both these examples were given by Montezuma to Cortés and sent by him to Charles V. They are now in the Museum für Völkerkunde, Vienna, where there is also a splendid feather-work mitre, one of a number which prove the survival of the craft after the Conquest.

The chief indigenous Aztec pottery is a thin, delicately made orange ware, decorated with fine cursive designs in grey or grey-black. Even this probably came from Puebla at an earlier date, when it was adopted by the Chichimecs of Tenayuca from whom it came to the Aztecs. The designs are mostly found on the insides of open bowls, many of them tripods on slender feet *(Ill. 55)*, and they go through a series of developments in detail. Four stages have been recognized and wrongly labelled Aztec I to IV, but in fact Stage II belongs to Tenayuca and only III and IV are Aztec. The first designs are stylized serpent heads within borders of concentric lines, scrolls, dots, etc., but by Stage III the central part of the design is generally abstract, though it may take other forms, for example a heraldic-looking eagle, and at Stage IV attractive naturalistic drawings of birds, fish, butterflies or insects may appear. This continued after the Conquest, and a remarkable fragment exists showing part of an Imperial double eagle with a crown over the heads. To Stage IV also belongs a fine glossy red ware bearing somewhat heavier but still delicate designs in black, typically running scrolls *(Ill. 56)*, or in some cases sections through conch shells, which were possibly a symbol of Quetzalcóatl. An imported ware was a remarkable, highly polished, glossy polychrome in red, black, yellow or orange, blue-grey and white, brought by trade or as tribute from Cholula *(Ill. 81)*. It has complex designs such as plumes, skulls and stone knives, which indicate a connexion with the religious cult.

56 Black-on-red cup supposed to be for drinking pulque. Aztec IV. Pulque is an intoxicating drink, made from the maguey plant, an aloe

57 *(left)* Black pottery spindle whorl. Aztec
58 *(centre)* Red pottery figurine perhaps representing Tonantzin, the Aztec goddess of motherhood
59 *(right)* Red pottery stamp showing a monkey. Aztec

Among smaller pottery products of local origin are mould-made figurines in dull monochrome ware in the form of gods, temples on pyramids, and human beings, but they have a mass-produced appearance and are lacking in inspiration *(Ill. 58)*. They contrast remarkably with the finer things, and they were probably made for use in humble households. More attractive are spindle whorls in black or grey ware *(Ill. 57)*, with designs engraved or in relief, and stamps showing a lively monkey *(Ill. 59)*. This and some eagles in relief on a spindle whorl are practically identical with contemporary examples from the Huastec region on the Gulf Coast *(Ill. 72)*.

Aztec art as a whole, whether indigenous or derived in varying degrees from outside, is full of strength and vigour. It pulsates with life, even though much of it is obsessed with death.

THE GULF COAST
The Classic and Post-Classic art of the Gulf Coast had a character of its own, although it both received influences from the highlands, especially Teotihuacán, and gave them to it. The key-notes of

70

highland art are angularity, order and a certain stiffness and severity, whereas the Gulf Coast is distinguished by softer modelling
and a great development of curvilinear scrolls. Covarrubias has
observed that both of them reflect the character of the modern
Indians, the highlanders being suspicious and reserved, and the
coast people extrovert and gay. The focus of the coastal plain
shifted northwards from the Olmec area to north and central Veracruz, but some stone sculpture, particularly the early Classic stelae
of Cerro de las Mesas in south-central Veracruz, can be related to
the Izapa style and through it to the Olmec. The area as a whole
is rich in sites and in the quality of its art, but few detailed studies
have been made and it is not yet possible to relate all its aspects
to one another.

What is now called the Classic Veracruz civilization can be exemplified by the important site of El Tajín in the north. It is an extensive ceremonial centre which is far from being completely excavated,
but it has the usual features of temple pyramids, platforms and
courts, besides at least seven ball-courts, suggesting that the ball-
game was particularly important there. In some form or other this
was played from Formative times (evidence for it at Tlatilco has
been given) to the Spanish Conquest. A heavy rubber ball was
propelled to and fro in a stone-walled rectangular court with transverse extensions at either end, so that it resembled a letter H with
an exaggerated crosspiece. The game had a religious character, and
the courts were closely associated with temples. In some cases it
involved the sacrifice of the leader of the losing side, and courts at
El Tajín have stone reliefs depicting the game, one of which shows
the sacrifice of a ball-player by others who are about to cut out his
heart under the eye of the death god (*Ill. 60*). These scenes are
framed and entangled in a maze of curvilinear scrolls which are
yet subordinate to a general rectangular arrangement. Similar
'inhabited scrolls', to borrow an analogy from Europe, are found on
stone discs used as the backs of pyrite mirrors, which occur both
locally and as far away as Kaminaljuyú in Guatemala, and unaccom-
panied scrolls of similar character are carved on stone vases from
the Ulua Valley in Honduras (*Ill. 63*).

60 Relief from ball-court, showing sacrifice of ball-player. Classic Veracruz style. El Tajín, Veracruz.

The number of players in the game, if it can be called one, varied widely; three a side was a usual figure among the Classic Maya, but the singles shown in sixteenth century codices and the teams of seven carved on the great Toltec Maya court at Chichén Itzá also spring to mind. They could strike the ball only with elbows, knees or thighs, and sometimes received serious injuries. Those in the codices are shown wearing only a loin-cloth, but earlier sculptured representations are heavily armoured. This protection sometimes took the form of a padded U-shaped leather belt with a separate upright piece in front, particularly on the Gulf Coast where it is shown on clay figurines (Ill. 61) as well as on the scenes mentioned

62 Graceful pale buff pottery head, the eyes decorated with pitch. Classic Veracruz style

White pottery figurine th some details picked t in black pitch, owing ball-player aring yoke and *palma*. assic Veracruz style. n José de Acatenco, ebla

63 Marble vase carved with scrolls of similar character to those seen in *Ill. 60*. Ulua Valley, Honduras

64 Finely-carved stone *hacha* showing head with dolphin crest.
Diorite, probably originally inlaid. Classic Veracruz style

65 Stone yoke in Classic Veracruz style, representing a stylized toad seen from above, covered with scrollwork patterns. Classic to Late Classic Period

above. The importance of this for our purpose is that some of the finest portable stone carvings from the area are considered to represent these things, those called yokes the belts *(Ill. 65)*, and those called *palmas* or palmate stones the uprights, while a third type, called from its shape *hacha* or axe *(Ill. 64)*, may depict an object attached to the back of the yoke. The carvings are crisp and very competent, and they may be exceedingly elaborate. Yokes have such subjects as a serpent head at either end and a human one in the middle, joined by the characteristic scrolls; *palmas* may have figures or scenes inhabiting a mass of scrolls (a well known example shows a sacrificed man with a gash in the chest, and another has interlace which is almost Anglo-Saxon in character); *hachas* frequently show heads, animals or birds.

A notable feature of El Tajín is the Pyramid of the Niches, which has six stages supporting a temple reached by one steep stairway. Each stage is faced with a row of stucco-covered square stone niches under an overhanging cornice, giving the pyramid a character unparalleled in any other area, and the stairway is broken at intervals by triplets of similar niches and confined by balustrades adorned by step frets. Like pyramids elsewhere, it was enlarged at some time and has an older one of similar type inside it. The main building activity here was in the late Classic Period, but the site seems to have survived the disturbances which marked the end of the period elsewhere, and flourished until about 1200. There are various features of Post-Classic character, such as representations of Eagle Knights, besides the death gods and scenes of human sacrifice, which may date from the later centuries of the occupation.

66 *(left)* Classic Veracruz hollow pale buff figurine of woman wearing skirt and *quexquemitl,* the eyes and ear ornaments painted with black pitch

67 *(above)* Classic Veracruz buff pottery ' laughing head '

68 Large hollow pottery figure of seated woman, wearing lip plug, with the eyes and nipples painted with black pitch. There was formerly a large pendant hanging from the necklace. From El Salto, Ignacio de la Llave, Veracruz. One of a number of remarkable recent discoveries near the boundary between Oaxaca and Veracruz, it shows a mixture of the Remojadas and Zapotec styles

Central Veracruz, near the city of that name, is known for the pottery figurines which abound at Remojadas and neighbouring sites. Starting in the Pre-Classic with entirely handmade ones, the art developed great exuberance in the Classic with the production of much more elaborate hollow figures, of which the faces alone may be mould-made *(Ill. 68)*. Among many varieties are women dressed in a modern Mexican fashion in skirt and *quexquemitl*, a pointed blouse *(Ill. 66)*, and they may have features such as the eyes or cheeks picked out with black pitch *(Ill. 62)*. The well-known 'laughing heads' with filed teeth *(Ill. 67)*, which show an expressiveness unique in America, are another product of the Classic in this area. They have broad, flattened heads and wear elaborate head-dresses, and the recent discovery of complete figures shows that they were dancing boys and girls wearing little but an abbreviated loin-cloth and narrow brassière. Gods such as Xipe, the flayed god, the death god and the wind god may be represented in a similar style, with some use of pitch to pick out details.

69 Black-on-cream 'teapot' vessel. Huastec. Post-Classic

Later pottery styles have been ascribed to the forbears of the modern Totonacs. They include a striking ware with designs in red and black, outlined by fine incised lines on an orange background, and a painted type showing leaping animals and other designs in orange on a black ground *(Ill. 70)*.

The Huastec zone lies to the north of those already dealt with, and includes the oil-producing region of Tampico. It is a Maya-speaking area, but is separated by a long distance and great differences in material culture from the main Maya country, so the two are believed to have been parted at a very remote time. A long succession going back beyond Formative times has been established but many of the most striking works of art belong to the Post-Classic stages, when strong influences were moving between Toltecs, Mixtecs and Huastecs. One result of this is the importance of Quetzalcóatl, a sign of which is the frequency of circular temples on conical 'pyramids', in which he was worshipped in his character of the wind god. A more particular instance is a remarkable red painted frieze at Tamuín, showing a procession of richly-dressed priests or gods in a strongly Mixtec-influenced style, which recalls in a general way the painted lintels at Mitla in Oaxaca although the composition is more crowded. On the other hand, there is a highly characteristic local pottery style, a soft cream ware decorated with bold patterns in black, which is best represented by the 'teapot' vessels with an upturned spout emerging from one side (*Ill. 69*). Carving in stone and shell flourished in the Huasteca, and Quetzalcóatl was frequently depicted in reliefs and shell plaques. Rather stiff standing limestone figures, partly covered with intricate patterns in low relief representing tattooing or textiles, are found here. Their head-dresses may end in a spike and are surrounded by a great semicircular halo, and some figures have a skull or a complete skeleton carved on the back. Of the same style is the well known 'adolescent', from Consuelo, near Tamuín, San Luis Potosí, a naked youth with about half his body painted or tattooed, a dwarf figure slung on his back, and pierced enlarged ear-lobes, which is generally recognized as one of the finest sculptures of the area (*Ill. 71*). At the very end of the story comes strong Aztec influence, shown by such things as clay stamps with Aztec monkey designs, and by the birds of prey depicted on finely-designed spindle whorls (*Ill. 72*).

70 Bowl showing orange leaping animals on black ground. Central Veracruz. Post-Classic

71 'The Adolescent'. Huastec statue with the body partly painted or tattooed, carrying an infant said to represent the sun on his back. Consuelo, near Tamuín, San Luis Potosí

72 Spindle whorl of cream-coloured pottery showing two birds of prey in relief

OAXACA

Oaxaca was occupied in Classic and Post-Classic times, and probably before, by the Zapotecs and Mixtecs. The Zapotecs lived chiefly in the middle of the State around the Valley of Oaxaca, and the Mixtecs in the hilly country to the north-west, whence they spread and took control of the Zapotec area in Post-Classic times.

Zapotec culture is known chiefly from the great hill-top centre of Monte Albán near the city of Oaxaca *(Ill. 74)*, which has already been mentioned in connexion with the Olmecoid *Danzante* carvings *(Ill. 13)*. This forms a great court, oriented approximately north-south and enclosed by pyramids and platforms, with a separate group of them in the middle. There is a great stairway at the north end, leading to a platform bearing the remains of two rows of circular columns, with a smaller sunken courtyard beyond. A stairway and buildings at the south end have not been fully excavated. Adjoining the north-east corner of the great court is a ball-court with sloping walls. All these buildings belong to the height of the Classic Period, called Monte Albán Stage III, dating from about A D I to 900. There is also an older spear-head shaped building oriented N E-S W, thought to be an observatory, near the central axis of the court towards the south end, which is ascribed to the late Formative Stage II, about 300 B C to A D I, and before this come the *Danzante* slabs (Stage I, about 700 to 300 B C), incorporated in a later group on the west side. From Stage II onwards there is continuity leading to a Classic florescence in Stage III, followed by decadence and abandonment of Monte Albán, except as a burial place, at the end of that stage. On the other hand, there is a break at the end of Stage I, which is ascribed to the arrival of new people bringing new features, perhaps as conquerors. The 'observatory' is faced partly with re-used *Danzante* slabs, and partly with slabs of its own date bearing incised glyphs, thought to denote places, each supported by an inverted head, perhaps to indicate its fall.

The pyramid and platform façades of Stage III are based on a variety of the 'slope-and-panel' type found at Teotihuacán, in which the slope is relatively much taller than it is there and the panel attempts to retain its importance by a heavy projecting frame enclosing its top and sides. A number of important stone-lined tombs have been found on the sides of the hill and generally under minor courts on the top. From being simple rectangular boxes in Stage I, they become chambers reached by stone stairways with small rectangular niches in side and back walls in Stages II and III, and in some cases the niches grow into transepts to produce a cruciform plan. They are roofed either with flat slabs, or with two sloping rows of slabs leaning against one another to form a ridge. Some are painted, a good example being Tomb 104. At the far end of this is a life-size face, possibly the maize god, opposite which on the side walls are two priests with the attributes of the maize god and possibly Xipe, accompanied by a macaw with a maize seed in its beak perched on a chest, heads probably glyphs, and numerals, painted in red, blue, yellow, black and grey. The tomb was sealed with a slab, carved on the inner side with an intricate pattern which appears to consist mainly of glyphs. The style of the carving resembles that of the paintings, and is distinguished by rather stiffly curvilinear scrolls, rounded forms and boldly drawn detail, which contrasts with the delicate and sometimes angular detail in the Classic paintings of Teotihuacán. There are other painted tombs, also carved stelae and other slabs showing one or more figures accompanied by glyphs, a frieze of warriors, and similar subjects, all in the same bold style.

Little indigenous work in jade has been recognized, and what there is is not of the first quality, but a number of fine objects which are thought to have been brought from the Olmec, Teotihuacán and Maya regions have been found. Among those tentatively

73 Mosaic mask of jade, with eyes and teeth of shell. Monte Albán II ▶

74 General view of Monte Albán, looking across the great plaza from the north

ascribed to the Olmec area is a splendid mosaic mask representing the bat god *(Ill. 73)*, made of 25 pieces of jade with eyes and teeth of white shell, which was found with a mask of pure Olmec style and many beads in a tomb of Stage II.

Zapotec pottery has some elements derived from the *Danzante* stage, a few Formative types of figurine, face urns, deep bowls with a vertical spout at the side, and above all the use of a mono-chrome grey clay, but many forms are new. Some of these show relationships to the Maya, but more to Teotihuacán, for example low flat-based bowls which may have tripod feet, and *floreros*, but peculiarly Zapotec are spool-shaped pot stands and, above all, funerary urns for placing in tombs or at their entrances. These

urns begin in Stage II as elaborate face jars, which may be a development from those of Stage I, in which a beautifully modelled head with a rich head-dress is applied to a cylindrical jar. Some of these must be portraits and some must represent gods. Finely modelled standing figures without urns may be found in the same tombs, but neither are common. In Stage III the head grows into a complete seated cross-legged figure with the hands resting on the knees, which covers the front of the urn entirely, and the head-dress and ornaments are greatly elaborated. Where the face is human it is standardized to a form which reveals a likeness to Teotihuacán figurines, showing that the individual has been submerged in his rank or office. The urns which represent gods, or

75 Funerary urn of grey pottery, representing Cocijo, the Zapotec rain god

men with god masks, most commonly show the attributes of Cocijo, the local rain god, with a forked serpent tongue and scrolls round the eyes *(Ill. 75)*. Others have their faces covered with a flayed face to represent Xipe, and others wear a head-dress made of a serpent face with its snout turned up and a great bush of quetzal feathers above to depict the maize god. Some of these are painted in rather soft and fugitive colours, such as red, green, blue and yellow, perhaps after firing. These urns become abundant at this stage, and the earlier ones are still finely modelled by hand, with some details cut out on the damp clay with a knife, but the later ones tend to be mass-produced in moulds.

76 Late Zapotec grey pottery vessel in form of eagle's claw. Monte Albán IV

Monte Albán was abandoned about A D 900, but whether this was connected with the Mixtec invasion is uncertain, because the known Mixtec sites in the area seem to be later. At any rate, the abandonment was followed by a stage of Zapotec decadence (Monte Albán IV), during which urns and other grey pottery were still made, a characteristic form being a small vase shaped like an eagle's claw (Ill. 76). Little is known of the early stages of Mixtec archaeology, although their painted books, dating from the fourteenth to the sixteenth century, contain genealogies from c. A D 600. There are many Mixtec sites in central Oaxaca, among which are Zaachila and above all the famous site of Mitla, some 25 miles east of the city of Oaxaca. There are five main groups of buildings at Mitla, of which the southernmost, consisting of a court with a pyramid on the east side and platforms on the others, all in very bad condition, is of Classic Zapotec date, but the remainder were built later, either by Mixtecs or by Zapotecs under Mixtec control. One of them, also in bad condition, is like the southern group in plan, though unquestionably later, but no details can be seen. The others are of the 'palace' type (dwellings of chiefs or priests), and some were still occupied when the Spaniards came. They have some features in common with those of Monte Albán, such as panels heavily framed at top and sides, but their general aspect is different. The Group of the Columns consists of two courts touching at one corner. The main one has buildings on three sides and is open to the south, and the other is similarly arranged but is open to the west. All the buildings are long and low, and the effect is accentuated by the elongated panels of stone mosaic with which they are decorated. These mosaics are highly characteristic of the Mixtec stage, each panel having a motif in relief in which zig-zag lines are prominent, such as a stepped hollow square or one of several varieties of step fret, many times repeated (Ill. 78). The main building of this group is on the north side of the north court, and consists of a large hall, with a row of plain columns along its long axis, which originally supported the roof beams. It leads into a small court behind, surrounded by rooms which are lavishly decorated with mosaics like those outside; the roof of one room has been restored with the aid of sixteenth century descriptions, and this brings home to us how dark they must have been. The south court is chiefly remarkable for two large cruciform stone-lined graves centrally placed beneath the north and east buildings and reached by stairways from the floor of the court. In both these courts the buildings are raised on low platforms and do not touch at the corners, which are therefore open. In the other two groups of buildings, there are no platforms and the buildings touch at the corners, so closing them, and it has been suggested that these two features may indicate a slightly later date. The better preserved of these groups consists of three courts joining one another along a north-south line, the southernmost containing the Colonial church, to erect which some of the buildings were destroyed. It is known as the Church Group. The lintels of some of the doorways are delicately painted with figure subjects in red in styles resembling those of the Mixtec painted books.

77 Mixtec stone figurines. Oaxaca

78 The stone mosaics in the hall adjacent to the court behind the Building of the Columns, Mitla

It has already been mentioned that there was an important centre of Mixtec art in Puebla, whence it is sometimes called Mixteca-Puebla, and that the influence of this extended far beyond its own area and was responsible for some of the best in Aztec art. The Mixtecs showed great skill in minor decorative arts, such as metal-work and other jewellery, small carvings of bone *(Ill. 86)* and hard stone *(Ill. 77)*, mosaic, and painting on walls, manuscripts and pottery. Large Mixtec sculptures are practically unknown, although signs of Mixtec influence on Aztec sculpture are evident as has been mentioned.

79 Drawing of Mixtec polychrome tripod pot, compared with interlocking head design on a Chimú textile from Peru

Most of the best surviving pre-Columbian manuscripts are of
Mixtec origin *(Ill. 83)*, and like others they take the form of screen-
folded strips of gesso-coated deerskin, painted on both sides and
protected by wooden covers. One group is concerned with genealogies, marriages, conquests, episodes in the lives of notables, and
the like, which are depicted by scenes after the manner of cartoons
showing richly-attired and brightly-painted figures in profile,
according to standardized conventions, accompanied by a wealth
of symbols, from which Professor Alfonso Caso and others have
extracted a vast amount of historical information. The chief colours
are yellow, brown, red, blue, green, grey and black. An important
feature which distinguishes Mixtec manuscripts is the use of a
sign like an A interlaced with a rectangle or oblong to denote the
365-day year, although it will be remembered that a very similar
sign was used architecturally at Teotihuacán and elsewhere in the
Classic Period. Individuals are identified by their name glyphs,
denoting the day of their birth in the 260-day calendar cycle. A

good example is given by the record of the life of a chief called 8-Deer, which has been pieced together from several books, where he is accompanied by a deer's head, the day sign Deer, and eight dots. He is shown performing sacrifices, conquering towns, capturing prisoners, marrying, having his nose pierced to receive a turquoise ornament denoting chieftainship, and finally being captured and sacrificed. The other group shows gods, associated calendrical matters, divination and mythological scenes. Mixtec wall paintings are of similar styles, but surviving examples are rare. The red-painted ones of Mitla have been mentioned, and there are polychrome ones at Tizatlán, Tlaxcala, which are comparable to the second group of books. A similar style is used for polychrome painting on pottery, and the colours are similar, except that the blues and greens are replaced by blue-grey, and orange is widely used. Among many beautiful examples in this style is a bowl from Zaachila, Oaxaca, with a bird perched on the lip *(Ill. 82)*. In addition to gods and figures like those on the manuscripts, there are symbols such as the section of a conch shell which denotes Quetzalcóatl, and angular patterns possibly derived from textiles, some of which are so like the interlocking head patterns of Peru

80 White Mixtec tripod bowl

81, 82 Two vessels of the Mixtec pottery generally called Cholula Polychrome. The one, from Cholula, Puebla *(above)*, has feathers, stone knives (in upper row), skulls (in bottom row) and other symbols. The other, from Zaachila, Oaxaca *(below)* has a humming bird on the rim

83 *(opposite)* Page from the Mixtec Codex ▶ Nuttall, showing scenes from the life of the Lady Three-Flint, who had previously given birth. Starting at top right, she offers various sacrifices, and ends at top left sitting with her husband the Lord Five-Flower in a house of government

as to suggest direct copying *(Ill. 79)*. (It would have been easy for Peruvian textiles to have been carried to Mexico, in spite of the lack of contacts between the peoples as a whole.) This ware, which has a high polish and is sometimes described as lacquered, is called Cholula Polychrome, after the great centre in Puebla where at least some of it was made. Very typical shapes are spheroidal bowls, standing on a fairly low pedestal base *(Ill. 81)* or pointed tripod feet, and they generally have a collar which is vertical or expands upwards. It is this ware which is often found also in Aztec contexts. Similar tripods are found in monochrome white pottery *(Ill. 80)*, and there is a plain grey ware in the Zapotec tradition, in which a typical form is a flat-based open bowl with tall tripod feet ending in eagle or snake heads. The Mixtec stage in Oaxaca is called Monte Albán V, although there was little use of that site except for burial.

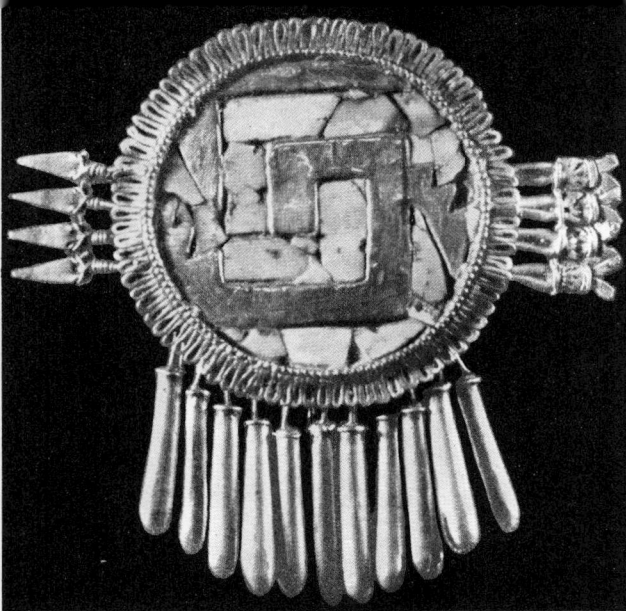

84 Mixtec jewel of gold
and turquoise. Yanhui-
tlán, Oaxaca

The richest hoard of Mixtec jewellery known was found by
Caso in Zapotec Tomb 7 at Monte Albán, which had been re-used
for a Mixtec burial. It contained jade, turquoise, rock-crystal,
shell, bone, gold, silver and copper, beautifully worked. A
gold pendant 4 $1/2$ inches high, shows a head with a rich head-dress,
issuing from a pair of plaques bearing two Mixtec year symbols
and the glyphs of the Mixtec year 11 House, its Zapotec equivalent
10 Wind, and the day 2 Knife. Another consists of 4 plaques
hanging from one another by rings, with danglers and 4 bells
below *(Ill. 85)*; the top plaque shows a ball-court with two players
and a skull between, the second is a solar disc, the third has a
moon glyph and the fourth an earth symbol. There was also a
thick gold mask of the god Xipe, 3 $1/4$ inches high. This elaborate
work was done by the cire-perdue process, still skilfully practised
in Oaxaca. A famous Mixtec jewel *(Ill. 84)*, from Yanhuitlán,
takes the form of a round gold shield with four arrows placed
horizontally behind it and little bells hanging below, which bears
a gold step fret set off by a similar form interlocking with it in
turquoise mosaic. A replica of this was presented by the Mexican
Government to H. M. the Queen as a wedding present. Returning
to Tomb 7, other treasures which it contained were gold rings
and nose ornaments, bead necklaces of shell, turquoise and large

94

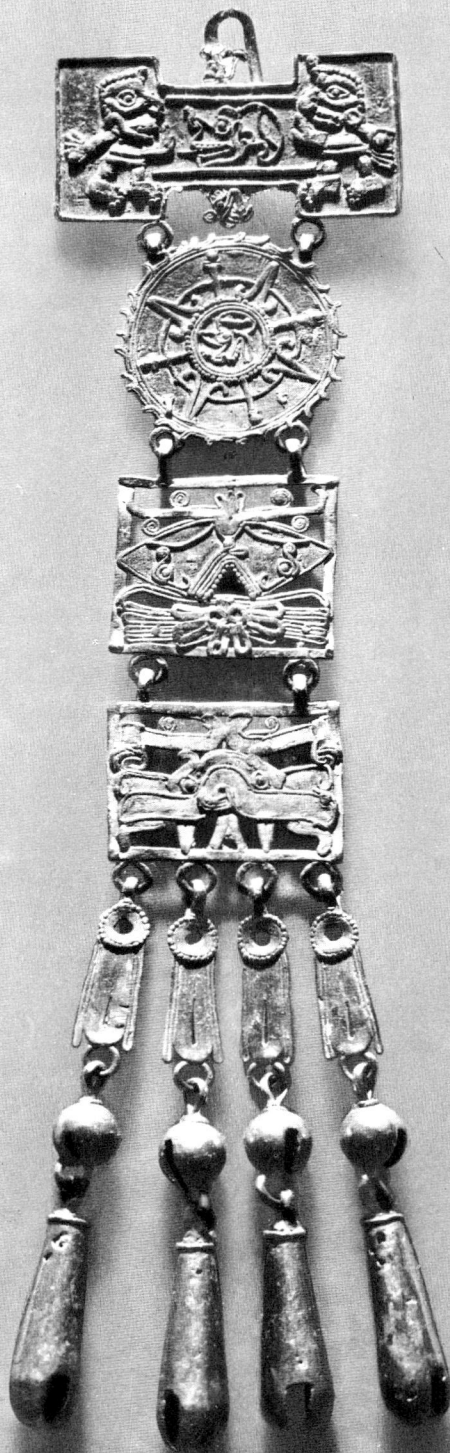

85 Mixtec gold pendant.
Tomb 7, Monte Albán

86 Two out of about 30 carved jaguar bones showing calendrical and other subjects. Mixtec. Tomb 7, Monte Albán

pearls, a crystal cup, and above all over 30 delicately carved bones *(Ill. 86)* showing the birth of a chief, animal heads, calendar signs in Mixtec style and other subjects, some of them set off by a background of turquoise mosaic. Among many other things were the remains of a human skull covered with turquoise mosaic, which supports the suggestion made in connexion with the Aztecs, that the famous 'Aztec' mosaics in the British Museum and elsewhere were Mixtec work.

THE WEST

Western Mexico is a large area with many facets; it lacks great ceremonial centres and stone monuments, and the chronology is little known in detail, but it is doubtful if the framework of Formative, Classic and Post-Classic has much meaning there, since work of Formative aspect may well have persisted through Classic times elsewhere. The chief artistic expressions in this area were

87 Bowls with red and black decoration on cream slip. Late Formative. Chupícuaro, Guanajuato

in pottery and small stone carvings, the latter particularly in Guerrero. The potters were concerned more with daily life than with the religions of other parts of Mexico, and we look in vain for the feathered serpent, Tlaloc, Xipe, Huitzilopochtli and the rest.

On the northern threshold of the area, at Chupícuaro, Guanajuato, a cemetery of late Formative date has produced a striking pottery style (*Ill. 87*), mainly bowls of various forms which may have pedestal or tripod feet, decorated with geometrical designs in red and black on cream. Stepped or zig-zag forms are characteristic. There are large hollow figurines similarly painted, as well as a small, well-modelled, solid type ('pretty ladies'), with large heads and applied details which include exaggerated slanting eyes (*Ill. 88*). They may have a touch of red or white paint here and there.

Further west is Michoacán, which in late post-Classic times was the home of the Tarascans, whose name has been mistakenly

88 Solid figurine, of red pottery, with touches of red and white paint. Late Formative. Chupícuaro, Guanajuato

89 *(centre)* Highly stylized face of dark green stone. Mescala or Guerrero style

90 *(right)* Olmecoid red pottery head from Iguala, Guerrero

given to much west Mexican art. At the time of the Conquest they were known as skilled metal-workers and jewellers, who produced such things as gold and copper bells, needles and fish hooks, and obsidian ear-plugs encrusted with turquoise mosaic of great delicacy. The local variety of pyramid was T-shaped in plan, with a central stairway on the cross bar and a round platform at the foot of the upright, on which was a circular shirne.

Guerrero is an area abounding in hard rocks, where communications are difficult and little is known about the archaeology. It has produced many small carvings in hard stones of many colours, including serpentine and jade, in the form of heads, masks, figurines, animals and temples, at least some of which are of Pre-Classic date. Details are shown by means of grooves or slits in preference to drilled holes, though these are not absent. The result is a highly characteristic local style with a marked abstract effect *(Ill. 89)*, which is sometimes called Mescala after a place near which many examples have been found, but Guerrero is preferable because it fits their range better. The masks and figurines may approach stone celts of various forms in outline, and some indeed are modified

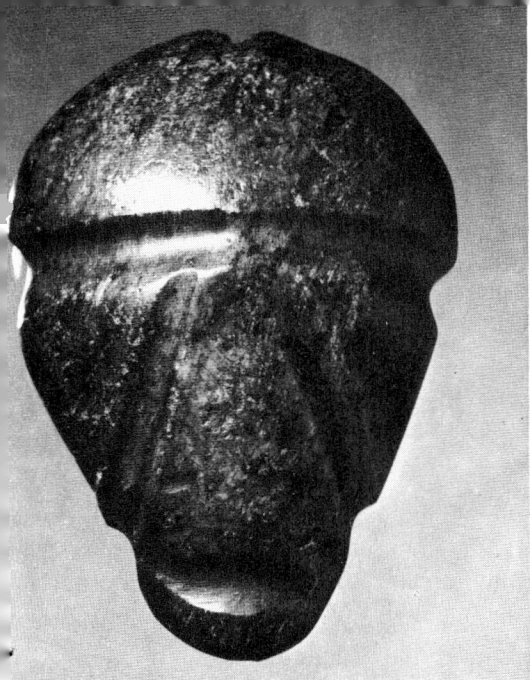

celts. In addition to those of the local style, there are figurines and masks of Olmec and Teotihuacán styles, and some hybrids which have been called Guerrero-Olmec or Guerrero-Teotihuacán, in many of which the local element quite overshadows any outside one. The true Olmec and Teotihuacán ones have given rise to much speculation as to whether Guerrero was the place of origin of these styles, but it is now thought more likely that the local specialist stone-carvers copied them from models perhaps of pottery, provided by outside clients. Indigenous pottery figurines with some Olmecoid features have been found (Ill. 90), but they are not really typical of that style.

The chief remaining areas in the west are the states of Nayarít, Jalisco and Colima, which can for our purposes be considered as a whole, although each has its special features. All are noted for their large hollow pottery figurines, which are vigorously hand-modelled and spontaneous in character. Those of Nayarít have an element of rugged caricature, with massive features and thin arms. There are individual figures and scenes of everyday life, such as a woman giving a man a drink, and there are groups of solid figures of smaller size, one of them showing a ball-game watched by an informal-looking audience. Into this class fall a number of examples of a man, in some cases highly stylized, lying on a bed and apparently bound to it *(Ill. 92)*. From this area also come some attractive pottery vessels modelled to represent vegetable forms *(Ill. 93)*. The figures of Colima *(Ill. 96)* are also concerned with daily life, but are softer and more rounded in contour than the rugged ones of Nayarít. They are smoothly finished and some have a red slip. Subjects include men and women sitting on the ground or on stools, standing, and drinking, also hunchbacks, warriors and prisoners. Most famous are the fat, hairless Colima dogs *(Ill. 94)*, which may be shown in a variety of natural attitudes, but some wear a mask and there is a pair dancing together, one fat and the other with the backbone showing and the ribs indicated by incised lines to give an effect of emaciation. Some of these dogs are jars, and they and some other jars have a narrow spout which emerges at a slant but is cut off horizontally. As in Nayarít, there are solid single figurines *(Ill. 95)* and groups, one of which has a ring of women dancing round three

91 Large red-slipped tripod jar, in the shape of a gourd, the feet in the form of birds, probably parrots. Colima

92 Man bound to a bed. Red on yellow slip. Nayarít

93 Red-slipped pot in the form of a flattened gourd. Nayarít

94 Jar in the form of a fat hairless dog of red ware. Colima

seated male musicians. There are large bowls with constricted mouths surrounded by flaring lips, and even the plain spherical ones give an effect of elegance, but many are modelled to represent fruits, snails, heads and other forms in a very attractive way *(Ill. 91)*. Jalisco is intermediate both in position and character. Good examples of the figure-modelling are given by armoured warriors brandishing a club or an arrow with an effect of purpose which draws the eye away from such details as the incompetent handling of the feet—a defect shared by many other figures in this region. All in all, the modelled work of these three states can justly be described as folk art.

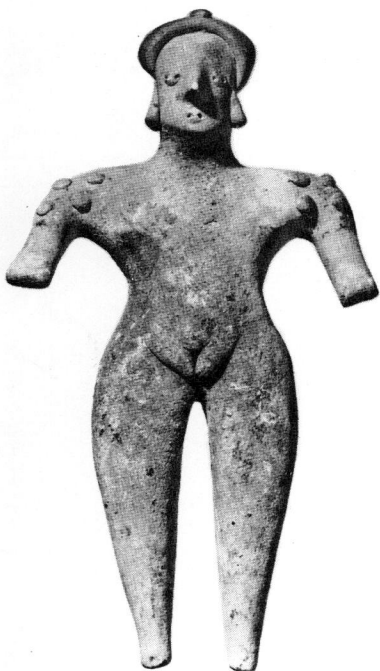

95 *(above)* Solid figurine of buff pottery. Colima

96 *(right)* Large hollow pottery figure of man blowing conch shell trumpet. Colima

CHAPTER TWO

The Maya

Formative and Classic

It is difficult to speak of Classic Maya art without some use of superlatives because it includes so much work of surpassing excellence. It is chiefly seen in a large number of ceremonial centres of different degrees of influence and importance, containing the usual elements of platforms, temple pyramids, palaces (probably the dwellings of rulers and priests), and ball-courts *(Ills. 98, 99)*, ranged around open spaces, with the addition of corbelled vaults *(Ill. 97)* as a roofing method and a large number of stelae, which are rectangular columns or slabs of stone. As in other areas, the emphasis is on the outsides of buildings and their disposition in space, for temples and rooms were small, dark and cramped in comparison with the volume of masonry used in their construction. The centres are distributed over a wide area, from north-west Honduras, through the lowland forests of Campeche and the Guatemalan Petén region, to the open plains of Yucatán, and they differ greatly in detail while sharing many features in common, just as their builders spoke several dialects of one language. There is reason to believe that each of the more important centres had its own sphere of influence which included a number of smaller ones, but that they themselves were independent of one another. Their rulers are thought to have been high priests, in friendly contact with one another and with Teotihuacán and other great centres, for reasons already given in the chapter on the Valley of Mexico. In addition they probably collaborated among themselves in devising and correcting their calendar, which was a great feature of Maya culture. It shared a 52-year cycle with other Mesoamerican civilizations, but added further terms and cycles which were used by no one else, including a count of days from a beginning far back in time. Many stelae were erected to mark period endings in this count, and the dates in it and in cycles moving

97 Copán, Honduras. Corbelled vault from the temple on the side of the ballcourt. Classic Maya

concurrently with it were recorded on them in hieroglyphic inscriptions of great complexity, which formed an important part of the decoration. The writing is not alphabetic, and insofar as it has been deciphered it can best be described as a form of pictorial rebus writing.

Maya art reflects the Maya character, and is serene, formal and impersonal. From its beginnings to the end of Classic times it was based on a stable culture, which was undisturbed by wars against peoples of similar status. There were constant rebuildings, involving enlargements and the burial of old pyramids under new, as in other Mesoamerican cultures, and there were changes in style. Nevertheless, there was a high degree of continuity. Stone sculpture was one of the chief media of expression, and the quantity which remains makes it particularly suitable as an index of stylistic development. It is seen typically on the stelae, on which the chief feature is a single figure of immense dignity, heavily loaded with ornament (*Ill. 100*). Whether these are gods,

98 (above) Copán, Honduras. Looking across the ball-court to the main plaza, with the Hieroglyphic Stairway in right foreground. Classic Maya. Note sloping walls of court

99 (below) Chichén Itzá, Yucatán. Post-Classic Maya ball-court. Note vertical walls

priests impersonating them, or rulers is uncertain, but most examples give the impression that the office mattered more than the man. Although the majority were erected to mark steps in the calendar, some stelae are now thought to have been put up at significant points in the life of a ruler. There is little impression of action and groups are rare, although minor figures on a smaller scale, such as attendants or prisoners, may accompany the principal one. Motifs and symbols are comparatively constant, changes occur slowly, there are few signs of individual artists' mannerisms and many of conformity to a rigid system. On the other hand, there are many differences between the various centres, thus the figures may be shown in very low flat relief, as on some thin, tombstone-like stelae at Tikal, and at the other extreme they may be in such high relief as to stand nearly clear of the stela, as in some at Copán. Some plain stelae may have been plastered and painted, and the intricacies of some of the later carved ones may well have been clarified by polychrome painting.

The length of the Classic Maya period was originally defined by the calendar cycles during which dated monuments were known to have been erected, namely from A D 317 to 889 in our calendar. Its beginning is further marked by the introduction of polychrome pottery and the corbelled vault as a roof structure, so there is reason to retain this date, although an earlier stela dated A D 292 and substantial ceremonial buildings several centuries older have been found at Tikal in the Petén. A notable Pre-Classic stone pyramid thickly coated with stucco was found within a later pyramid at Uaxactún, also in the Petén, and this was decorated with large stucco masks of Olmec affinities, which supports the idea already mentioned that Maya art was at least partly rooted in the Olmec.

Maya sculpture has been the subject of an important study by Miss Tatiana Proskouriakoff, to which any discussion is bound to owe much. She shows that the earliest stelae are related to other styles, like Izapa, and have the main figure with head and feet in profile and the body partly turned towards the viewer, an attitude seen also in miniature on the famous jade plaque, the

100 Stela D, Quiriguá, Guatemala. Showing majestic figure of a god or ▶ ruler. Late Classic Maya, probably erected A D 766

Leiden plate. Early in the Classic, in the fifth century, the same attitude persists but the dress and ornaments become more specifically Maya, and attributes like the serpent bar, a kind of sceptre supported on both arms, are developed. There was a gap from 534 to 593 when scarcely any dated stelae were dedicated, after which there was an increasing interest in detail at the expense of the main subject. The figure stands with his body facing the viewer, with both feet splayed out, but his head is generally in profile at first. Elaboration of detail continued to increase, but the subject remained static until about 750, after which for another 60 years came what is called the Dynamic Phase, in which an effect of movement is produced on some carvings largely by means of asymmetrical poses, accompanied by increasingly large feathered head-dresses and other appendages. After 810, decadence set in and was marked by excessive flamboyance—sandals with great sprouting tassels which would make it impossible to walk, and so on. This continued until the abandonment of many of the great centres by the end of the ninth century.

Each of the greater centres excelled in some feature of architecture or sculpture, and in Yucatán and Campeche are architectural styles which extend over a considerable area. Tikal, which is the largest of them all, is known for the great height of its pyramids, the towering, intricately carved roof combs of the temples which crown them, and the carved wooden lintels over the temple doors. The fine series of high relief stelae for which Copán in Honduras is distinguished has already been mentioned, and at Quiriguá in Guatemala, not far away, the figures are constrained within the rectangular shape of the column, from which the head looks out like the face on a mummy case. Here is the tallest stela of all (35 feet high), and there are four great boulders whose whole surface is covered with elaborate carving thought to represent a sky monster, with a richly-dressed human figure sitting between its jaws. Piedras Negras, also in Guatemala, is outstanding for the beauty of its carving both on stelae and on glyph-bordered wall panels, one of which shows a ruler on his throne surrounded by attendants. Palenque is beautifully placed on rising ground

101 Temple of the Sun, Palenque, Chiapas, with the Temple of the Inscriptions in the background, showing elaborate roof comb and remains of stucco relief decoration. Late Classic Maya, probably dedicated A D 692

against a background of tree-covered hills, looking out north-wards over the plain of Chiapas (*Ill. 101*). Its low relief limestone panels and its stucco reliefs are unsurpassed in dignity of form and delicacy of execution (*Ills. 102-104*). The late Classic buildings of the Puuc, the hilly region of south-western Yucatán and part of Campeche, will serve as an example of a regional style. The buildings are of lime concrete veneered with thin, well-cut stone slabs, sometimes forming an ornate mosaic, and there are more palace-type buildings in proportion to the number of temple pyramids than there are in the Petén.

102, 103 Full figure numerical glyphs, part of an inscription from the Palacio at Palenque, Chiapas. This type which is rare shows a time period or day on the right, supported by a number on the left. Both are regarded as gods. Limestone. Late Classic Maya.

104 (opposite) Low relief limestone carving from a slab covering the coffin in the tomb under the Temple of the Inscriptions Palenque, Chiapas. It shows a reclining figure from which sprouts a tree or plant. Late Classic Maya.

105 (opposite) House of the Turtles at Uxmal, Yucatán. Plain façade pierced by three doorways : fluted frieze below a row of small turtles. Lime concrete veneered with thin stone slabs. Late Classic Maya

106 (above) Palace of the Governor, Uxmal, Yucatán. Façade with heavy decorated frieze pierced by two tall corbelled ' arches '. Late Classic Maya, Puuc style

Uxmal is among the foremost examples of this style. It is noted for its long façades, in which a comparatively low plain wall, broken by a series of doorways, is crowned by a higher frieze covered with intricate mosaic decoration. These are well seen in the 'Nunnery' court, and in the fine Palace of the Governor (Ill. 106), also known for two exceptionally tall corbelled 'arches' which break the long line of the façade. Contrasting with these is the plain-looking House of the Turtles (Ill. 105), with a frieze adorned only with vertical fluting, above which is a row of small turtles. Part of the decoration of the ' Nunnery ' court consists of masks of the long-nosed rain god, similar to those which are seen in profusion both on late Classic and Post-Classic buildings at the great centre of Chichén Itzá in northern Yucatán.

The Maya were adepts at the use of stucco, which was widely used for floors and the decoration of buildings. At Palenque, where it reached its highest level, there are fine panels in relief showing figures or groups on the temples, and a procession of richly-dressed priests adorns the secret tomb which was found buried beneath the Temple of the Inscriptions. The same tomb contained two magnificent stucco heads modelled in the round

113

and decorated with red paint (*Ill. 107*), with the typical long Maya noses and retreating foreheads and plumed head-dresses. Traces of paint are often found on modelled stucco, and much of the decoration on buildings was probably coloured; for example, polychrome stucco masks have recently been found on late Pre-Classic buildings at Tikal.

From painted modelled plaster it is but a step to mural paintings. Traces of polychrome paintings have been found in many places —Uaxactún, Palenque, Tikal and others—but the most remarkable come from three corbelled vaulted rooms making up a building at Bonampak in Chiapas (*Ill. 110*). The paintings are obscured by a coating of stalactite and we owe our knowledge of them to careful copies made by two artists under great difficulties. Opinions differ as to whether they were painted on dry plaster or in true fresco. They form a sequence showing a great ceremony; the robing of the priests and an orchestra, a raid on an inferior tribe to get prisoners (not a war between equals), their arraignment and sacrifice, and finally a dance and blood-letting ceremony by the high priest and his family. They show a wide range of colours, blue, green, black, white and a number of shades of red, brown and yellow. Although they were done about A D 800, during the Dynamic Phase of sculpture, their liveliness and realism far exceed anything which was attempted in stone. Even the attitudes and facial expressions of the participants reflect the scene they appear in; they are fierce in the fighting, and dignified and unmoved at the sacrifice, the collapse of the dead prisoner is vividly shown, the next in turn raises his hands in supplication and the rest squat helplessly below. It is to their outlines that these paintings owe most of their expressiveness, and it has been well said that they are best regarded as coloured drawings. The artists worked within certain conventions : thus heads are always shown in profile, which occasionally results in such anatomical absurdities as twisting the neck through 180°, and the feet are nearly always in the stiff splayed or sideways positions of the stelae. There is no interest in any life forms except human ones, and depth is shown only by partial superpositions, sometimes at different levels.

107 Head of a young man wearing an elaborate plumed head-dress. Stucco ▶ with traces of red paint. Late Classic Maya. Burial chamber under the Temple of the Inscriptions, Palenque, Chiapas

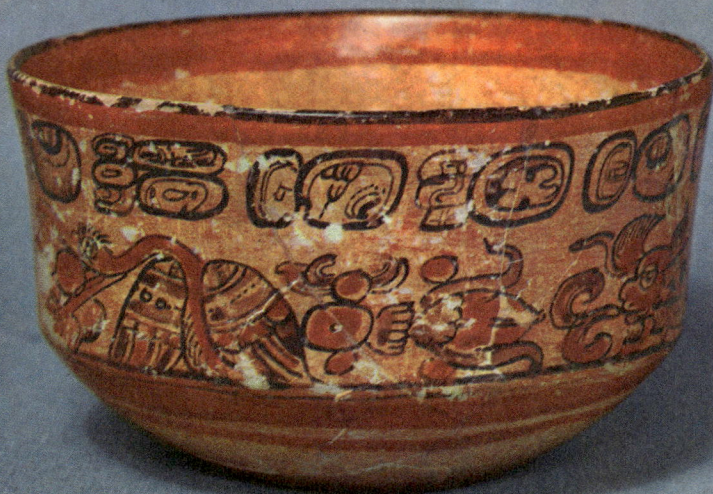

108 Bowl decorated with marine monsters and stylized glyphs. Orange and black on buff slip. Late Classic Maya. Caracol, British Honduras

109 Design from a vase showing priests and dignitaries in full costume. Red, yellow and black paint on buff slip. Late Classic Maya. Chama, Guatemala

110 Wall painting *(copy)* depicting a raid on a inferior tribe to get prisoners. Polychrome paint on plaster (perhaps true fresco). Maya, *c.* A D 800. Bonam-pak, Chiapas

111 Polychrome vase showing kneeling figures with head-dresses above a band of glyphs.   Classic Maya

In contrast are the faces already mentioned and above all the hands, which show a multitude of gestures and almost seem to speak.   All in all these paintings are among the greatest works of art in ancient America, and can, in their own way, bear comparison with wall paintings anywhere.

Pottery is another medium for polychrome painting *(Ills. 108, 109)*; reds, browns and yellows predominate, with the addition of black and sometimes blue, the same as that of the Bonampak paintings, of which the exact nature still baffles investigators.   Painting is found on vessels of many shapes, mostly some form of plate or bowl.   There are open bowls, which may have a flange low down on the outside, vertical-sided tripod bowls with slab feet like those of Teotihuacán, shallow open tripods *(Ill. 111)*, deep cylinders, pear-shaped jars which may have a ring base, and many others. Some basal-flanged bowls and some Teotihuacán-type tripods have

112 Tripod bowl of thin black ware with incised designs, including a bird which is also modelled on the cover. Early Classic Maya. From the painted tomb at Tikal, Guatemala, A D 457

low conical lids topped by a bird or animal *(Ill. 112)*. Painted scenes include processions, scenes of offering and other ceremonies, accompanied by glyphs which in many cases appear to be merely decorative and without meaning. Some of these shapes, including the Teotihuacán-type tripods, may be covered with painted stucco, the 'paint cloisonné' decoration already described for Teotihuacán itself, or may be made in polished black ware with delicate incised designs. Most of the decoration is Maya in character, but some instances recently found at Tikal show strong Teotihuacán influence. These are some of the more notable decorated pottery types, but there are many others, and figurines were also made. Solid hand-made ones, some of them crude but others well-fashioned and already showing Maya facial characteristics, belong to the late Formative Period *(Ill. 114)*. The other main group dates from the late Classic and comes largely from the Mexican states of

113 Whistle figurine in the form of a seated man wearing elaborate plumed head-dress. Grey pottery, mould-made, the necklace painted blue. Late Classic Maya. Jaina

114 *(right)* Red pottery female figurine, wearing large necklace and ear-spools. Hand-modelled with touches of red and white paint and applied details. Late Formative Maya

Campeche and Tabasco. These are mould-made, many of them hollow, and of fine quality. Notable examples come from Jonuta, the island of Jaina, and Palenque. Some of these figures are also whistles *(Ill. 113)*.

The Classic Maya showed great skill in a number of minor arts. The nature of their textiles and feather work can be deduced only indirectly because none have survived, but judging from sculptural representations they wove elaborate patterns. They also engraved complicated scenes with great delicacy on bones, of which a great deal has been learnt from recent finds at Tikal. Most important was jade, the most precious material known to the Maya. To judge from grave offerings and sculptures, a dignitary was loaded with it. Elaborate bead collars with pendants, large ear ornaments, belt ornaments, anklets and beaded kilts were all used. Jade is a hard intractable material to shape with stone tools and abrasives, but the Maya worked it with great skill. The Leiden plate, with its delicate incised decoration, is an early example. Heads and masks used as pendants, figurines, beads and ear ornaments were carved in the round, and many plaques with heads or groups in low relief were made *(Ill. 115)*. A prominent part of an ear ornament was a funnel-shaped flare, whose neck passed through the lobe and was held by a backing plate; some were adorned with a tassel in the middle and some formed the seating of a cylindrical bead. Such flares had other uses, and one of the finest examples *(Ill. 116)*, from Pomona,

British Honduras, which is 7 inches in diameter, may have been a belt ornament. It has incised glyphs, so far not read. It is curious that some finely worked low relief plaques are asymmetrical or even irregular in outline, as though the makers were only interested in the surface.

Finally, great dexterity was shown in the shaping of flint. Caches of flint objects are found buried under Maya monuments, and these take the form of finely shaped blades, crescents, discs and curious irregular objects, some of which are thought to have been heads of ceremonial staves. The outlines of some of these incorporate human profiles *(Ill. 117)*.

117 Eccentric flint flaked to incorporate human profiles. Perhaps the head of a ceremonial staff. Maya. Unprovenanced

15 Seated dignity or god wearing elaborate headdress. Pale green jade plaque, carved and drilled in low relief and highly polished. Classic Maya. Unprovenanced

16 Large annular flare; glyphs on a plain surface. Earspool shape, but perhaps belt ornament. Dark green jade, engraved and highly polished. Proto-Classic Maya (Late Formative). Pomona, British Honduras

118 El Castillo at Chichén Itzá, Yucatán. General view of the pyramid crowned with a temple. Post-Classic Maya

Post-Classic

Beginning with Copán early in the ninth century, the Maya ceased to erect dated stelae at one centre after another during the next 75 years or so, and the hierarchy at least abandoned them to the forest, though in some cases the peasants remained in the neighbourhood. Some sites in Yucatán, notably Chichén Itzá, were reoccupied in the tenth century after a short interval, and at others such as Uxmal it is difficult to draw a line between Classic and Post-Classic. At Chichén Itzá itself some late Classic buildings were modified in the Post-Classic, and many new ones were built. There were still pyramids crowned with temples (El Castillo at Chichén is a splendid example, *Ill. 118*) and ball-courts, but the character of the wall-painting and sculpture changed and spacious colonnaded buildings of a new type were set up. The sculpture in particular was very closely related to that of Tula, as has already been hinted. There is a new preoccupation with violence and death, seen in reliefs showing rows of skulls on poles *(Ill. 119)*

119 Relief showing human skulls on poles. Shallow carving on the *tzompantli* or skull rack. Post-Classic Maya. Chichén Itzá, Yucatán

and eagles and jaguars eating human hearts. The worship of the feathered serpent is seen in his representation as a square column of Toltec type, with his head on the ground and his rattlesnake tail in the air, where it was used to support a lintel *(Ill. 120)*. Of the same Toltec origin are the Chac Mools, reclining stone figures bearing a stone bowl on the stomach. The great ball-court, with its painted temples, has new features such as vertical sides in each of which is a stone ring, and if a team was lucky or skilful enough to propel the ball through it, the result was an outright win. The consequences can be guessed from a series of stone reliefs on the walls of the court at ground level, in which two heavily armoured teams of seven players are seen facing one another. The leader of one has dropped on one knee, and from his neck sprouts a luxuriant plant surrounded by six snakes; the leader of the other holds a stone knife in one hand and his opponent's head in the other. The scene is repeated six times. It has been inferred that the game was a fertility rite in which the victim's blood fertilized the ground.

Notable wall paintings have been found here, although few details now survive in a recognizable condition. They do not approach those of Bonampak in dignity and composition, but are

124

120 Pillar in the form of a feathered serpent, its rattle snake tail formerly supporting the lintel of the temple entrance. Post-Classic Maya. Temple of the Warriors, Chichén Itzá, Yucatán

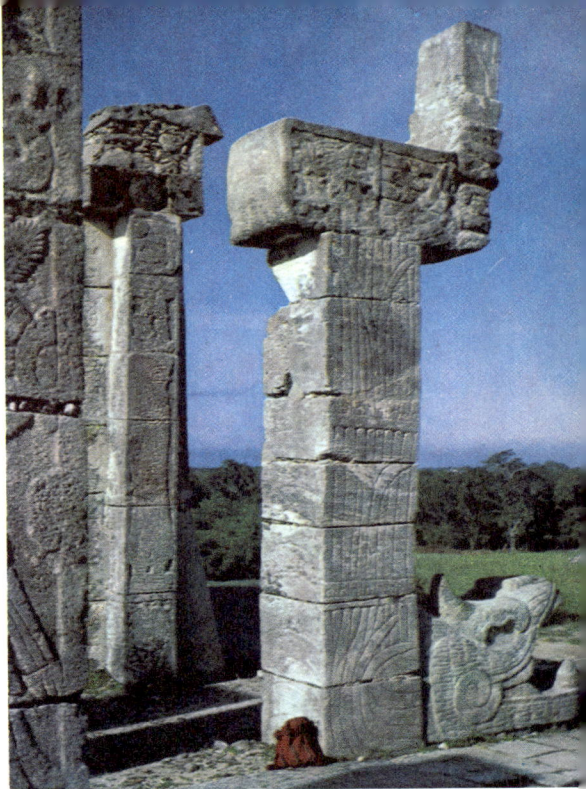

121 Wall painting of a waterside village *(copy)* showing various activities and canoes carrying warriors. Polychrome on plaster. Post-Classic Maya. Temple of the Warriors, Chichen Itzá, Yucatán

full of ethnographic interest. There is a waterside village with people sitting or moving among the houses and canoes carrying warriors in front *(Ill. 121)*, and an attack on a Maya village by Toltecs, in which a large area is covered with little warriors fighting in great confusion.

For the first time metal comes into the picture. Water is found on the dry plateau of Yucatán only in deep holes called *cenotes*, formed by underground solution of the limestone, and the Great Cenote at Chichén, which is a deep pool surrounded by vertical cliffs 65 feet high, was a place of sacrifice into which people and valuable things were thrown. Dredging of this has yielded, among many other things, several finely-embossed gold discs showing war between Toltecs and Mayas, culminating in one on which a victim is killed by the Mexican method of cutting out the heart. The gold came from Panama, but the workmanship is Mexican.

Chichén Itzá ruled Yucatán for about 200 years, after which it was displaced by Mayapán, some miles to the west. Like many Post-Classic centres this was a walled town, and the ceremonial nucleus was a very pale reflection of the older ones. Toltec influence had faded away and the Maya emerged again as rulers of their own people, but they retained militaristic habits and did not recover their artistic skill. Excavation of Mayapán has revealed a sorry state of affairs—building of poor quality with ill-fitting stones and the defects made good with plaster, little decorated pottery except mass-produced incense burners varied only by paint and minor applied details, and a dearth of jade and other beautiful objects. The best masonry was found not in religious buildings but in chiefs' houses outside the nucleus. Mayapán was sacked in a revolt in about 1450, but the warring states which succeeded it did nothing to arrest the artistic decline.

CHAPTER THREE

A Glance to the North

The art of the ancient inhabitants of North America suffers by comparison with that of Mesoamerica because it lacks monumental sculpture and had comparatively little which can be regarded as architecture. This is not to say that the peoples of the area had no artistic ability, for in some areas they produced fine examples of small carvings, pottery and even metalwork, though this came exclusively from naturally occurring metals and not from ores. A few examples will give some idea of what was achieved.

Temple pyramids surely inspired by Mexico were built more or less regularly round courts in the region of the middle Mississippi Valley after about A D 1000, but they are of earth and have weathered to nondescript shapes. To the north, mainly in Wisconsin, Minnesota, Illinois and Iowa, there are large earthworks in the shape of animals and birds, apparently dating from the second half of the first millennium A D. Some of the great 'apartment houses' in the southwest (mostly Arizona, Colorado and New Mexico), dating from about A D 1000-1300, with their numerous rectangular rooms and sacred circular *kivas*, have an impressiveness derived either from their setting beneath or clinging to the sides of great towering cliffs, or in the open from their size and regular lay-out. Wall paintings have been found in some of the *kivas*, showing gods and ceremonies, many of which can be interpreted in the light of surviving practices, largely concerned with weather control. They are painted in a wide range of mineral colours on mud plaster, and show angular schematized figures like modern Katchina dolls from the same area, animals, fish, jars with rain pouring out, arrows denoting lightning, and so on. They were not meant to last, and the fragmentary state of many is due not only to age but to frequent replastering and to deliberate destruction when a ceremony was finished.

122 Five ornamental geometrical forms, including scrolls and a swastika. Native copper, beaten, cut and annealed. Hopewell Culture. Ohio

Many minor arts are best illustrated by the Hopewell Culture (about 300 BC to AD 300), which has richly furnished burials under large mounds, chiefly in Wisconsin, Illinois, and especially Ohio. The grave goods include copper, stone, pottery and mica. Native copper was cut, beaten and annealed to form head-dresses with antlers, ear-spools, and plaques in the form of animals, fish, birds, crescents, swastikas and complex geometrical forms, some of them for sewing to robes *(Ill. 122)*. Sheets of mica were cut into silhouettes of bear or bird claws, hands and headless human beings *(Ills. 124, 125)*. There are finely-carved stone pipes, in which the bowl is a naturalistic figure, usually a bird or animal *(Ill. 123)*. Delicately-flaked obsidian knives and spear-heads, too large and fragile for use, were also deposited in the graves.

123 Three tobacco pipes with bowls in the form of marmot, frog, and snake. The front views show smoke channel. Steatite, carved, with some shell inlay. Hopewell Culture. Ohio

124 *(opposite)* Two silhouettes showing mutilated human figures. Cut from a thin sheet of mica. Hopewell Culture. Ohio

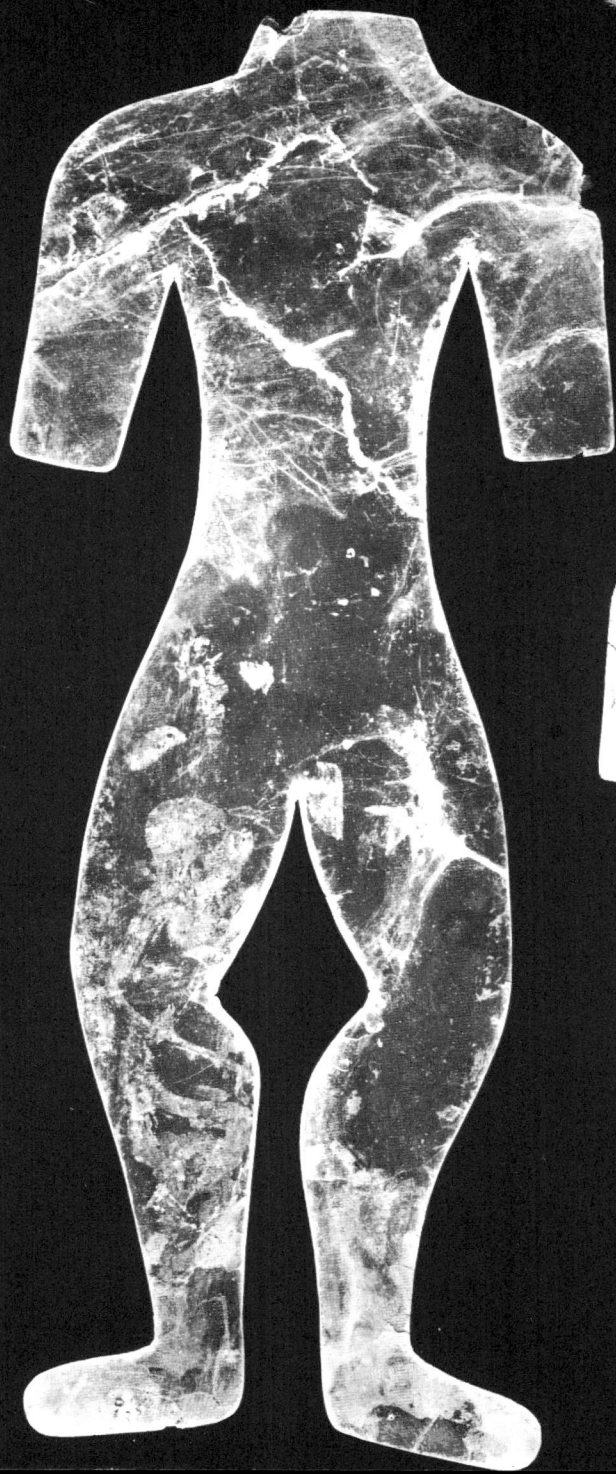

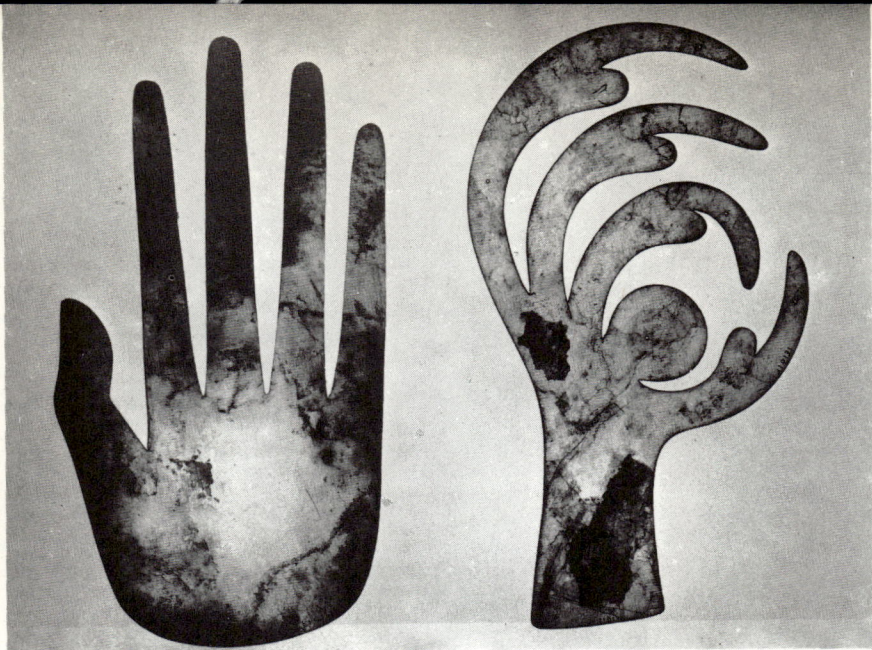

125 Two silhouettes of a human hand and an eagle's claw. Cut from a thin sheet of mica. Hopewell Culture, Ohio

Further south and later in date, in the Mississippi Valley and the South-East, are engraved or pierced shell discs, and pierced and embossed copper ones, bearing designs such as faces with weeping eyes, crosses, and eagle warriors carrying trophy heads, which, like the pyramid-building cultures with which they are connected, show Mexican influence, probably from the Huastec region, despite the great distance and the lack of connecting links.

Many works of art in carved wood were undoubtedly made, but few have been preserved. The best evidence about them comes from a find of late prehistoric date at Key Marco on the Gulf Coast of Florida *(Ill. 126)*, where the wood had been preserved by continuous immersion in water, but unfortunately it was found before the invention of modern methods of preservation and most of the objects have shrivelled up. Many of them were painted. There were beautiful animal and bird heads, masks, spear-throwers and other weapons, boxes and panels painted with animals and birds.

126 Deer-head mask, with large leather-hinged ears. Carved wood, originally painted. Late Prehistoric. Key Marco, Florida

127 Pottery bottle with swirl design, painted red and white. Middle Mississippi Period, after AD 1000.

128 Bottle with concentric linear designs. Pottery with burnished black slip, incised after firing. Middle Mississippi Period, after AD 1000. Caddo

129 Black-on-white bowl, showing contrast between the areas of solid colour and hatching. Pueblo III, c. 1050-1300. Mesa Verde, Colorado

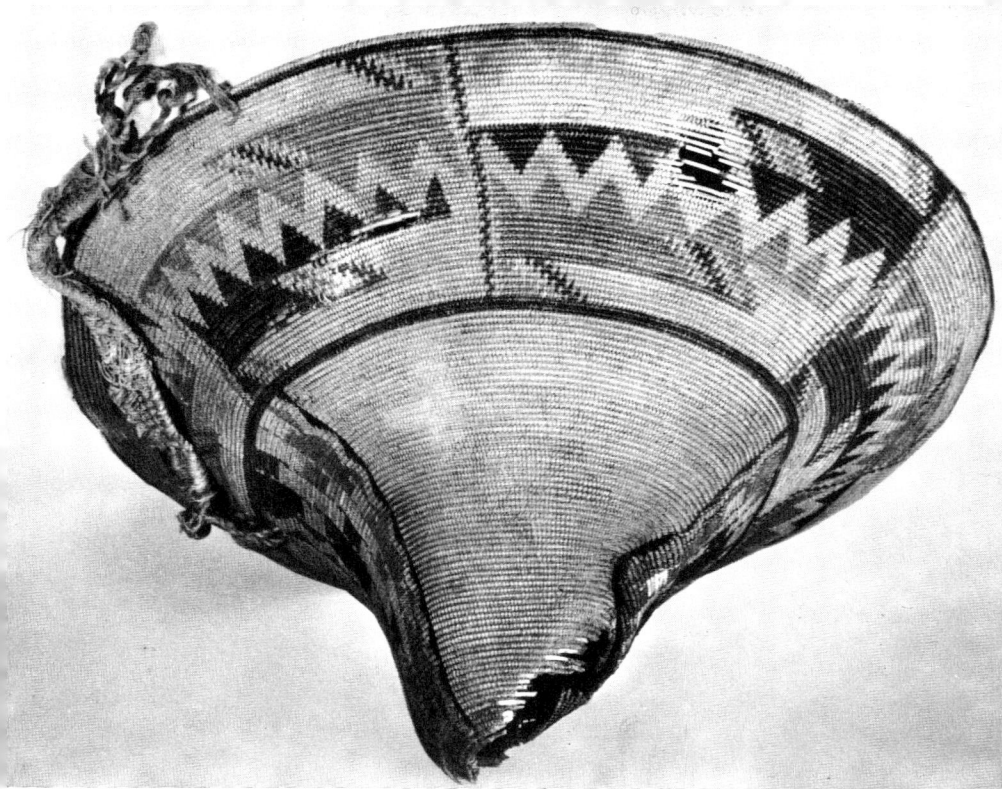

130 Coiled burden basket with geometrical designs, in red and black on natural ground. Basketmaker III, AD 500-700, Canyon del Muerto, Arizona

Attractive pottery was made in many places. Most wares are in one colour, with decoration by incision, stamping and the like, and occasionally modelling. Painting is confined to a few areas; it is sometimes found in the Mississippi area *(Ills. 127, 128)*, but it can best be exemplified by the Southwest. In both these areas the idea but not the designs may have come from Mexico. In a large part of the Southwest, white-slipped jars, bowls and handled mugs decorated with a great variety of intricate, mainly angular, geometrical designs in black, were made between about A D 700 and 1300 *(Ill. 129)*. At the same time, and even earlier, similar designs were worked in basketry *(Ill. 130)*. Between 1000 and 1200, a particularly striking variety of black-on-white pottery

131 Bowl, stylized turtle within a geometrical border. Pottery, black paint on white slip. A hole has been punched in the centre, ceremonially 'killing' the dish for burial with the dead. AD 1000-1200, New Mexico

132 Sikyatki Polychrome bowl, incomplete, painted in black and red on yellow. Ruin 4, Horn House, Moki Reservation, Arizona

133 Vase with geometrical and scroll designs in compartments. Black and red paint on buff slip. *c.* AD 1300-1450. Chihuahua, Mexico

was made in the Mimbres Valley of New Mexico *(Ill. 131)*, which is marked by great delicacy in drawing and the introduction of life forms. Men, groups, animals, fish and insects are placed in the middle of a bowl, which may also have a geometrical border of great intricacy. The central design is all too often marred by the habit of 'killing' the bowl by punching out a disc when it was buried with the dead. Between about 1300 and 1450 another distinctive type was made in the Mexican state of Chihuahua *(Ill. 133)*. This is decorated in black and red on buff, mainly in geometrical designs, and the delicacy of the drawing suggests a Mimbres strain in its ancestry, but many of the vessel shapes, including effigy jars, are different. Back in Arizona and New

Mexico, the black-on-white gave place after 1300 to other types and colours. Black-on-red varieties already existed in the area, and white was added to these, and in some parts matt black was replaced by a black to brownish-green glaze paint unique in America. Yellow and orange backgrounds were also used. Among many varieties is a beautiful ware, Sikyatki Polychrome *(Ill. 132)*, in which conventionalised animal designs are painted in sweeping curves of black and red on large yellow bowls and jars.

CHAPTER FOUR

Peru

As a centre of high civilization in the New World Mesoamerica was rivalled only by Peru, which with highland Bolivia forms a unit sometimes called the Central Andes. The whole area has many cultural features in common, and at two periods, and to a lesser extent a third, it was united artistically by the spread of what is called a horizon style, but at other times there was a good deal of variety in different districts, which is seen particularly in pottery styles, and this was to a considerable extent the result of broken and complex topography. The area falls into three zones, of which one, the forested lowlands east of the Andes, can be ignored here because it has produced no artistic developments of any consequence; indeed there were no civilizations which would be likely to support any. Of the other two, the coastal plain is a narrow strip of rocky and sandy desert, where it seldom rains in some parts and never in others. It is crossed from east to west by a series of irrigated valleys running from mountains to sea, which were the cradles of many Peruvian cultures; the deserts separating them were formidable barriers, but some of the more powerful coastal states were, at different times, able to group several of them under their rule. To the east of the coastal plain lies the zone of the high Andes, with its snow-covered peaks, bleak plateaux, high passes and deeply-cut valleys, constituting obstacles to communication which led to much diversity in art styles. It is convenient to break both coast and highlands down into northern, central and southern sections. The central coast extends from just south of the Casma Valley to just south of Lima, with the northern and southern sections on either flank. Owing to lack of knowledge the corresponding highland sections are less well defined; the boundary between north and central sections is at about the same latitude as the coastal one, but that between the central and southern highlands is roughly 2 degrees south of the coastal boundary, between Pucára, some distance north-west of Lake Titicaca, and Cuzco, and the southern section extends far further south to cover the Bolivian highlands.

The chronology of the Peruvian area was briefly mentioned in the introduction, and it must now be amplified. For our purposes the sequence begins about 2500 B C during a Pre-Ceramic Period, long before anything deserving the name of art was known in Mesoamerica. A remarkable art style is expressed at this time chiefly in the unpromising medium of twined cotton textiles, found in such a faded and tattered condition that years of patient work have been necessary to reveal the patterns. Their makers lived on the coast, and about forty of their settlements have been found, some of them in places which now appear very dry but which yielded sufficient water for their limited needs. They lived largely on sea lions, shell-fish and fish, and cultivated a few plants, including the cotton used in their textiles. The beginning of the Formative is hard to define satisfactorily, but it may be put arbitrarily at about 1800 B C when the first pottery is known in the north highlands, although important temples were present earlier. There was little change in the life of the coast people until the arrival about 800 B C from Mesoamerica of new influences and possibly new people, bringing jaguar worship and a more productive form of maize. The art style connected with this marks the Chavín horizon, which spread widely through the coast and into the north highlands. This is the limited horizon style mentioned above. The Formative Period lasted until about A D 250, when it gave place to what it is convenient to call the Classic Period, although its character is very different from that of the Mesoamerican Classic. It was, for instance, a time at which fortresses were built and the importance of war and warriors is clearly shown in the art, and is deducible from the archaeological record. As has been said in the introduction, art lost in vigour what it gained in technical perfection at this time. The Classic Period was brought to an end between about 750 and 950 by the expansion of influence from Tiahuanaco in the south highlands.

It is thought that this first affected the important site of Huari in the Mantaro Basin, and then spread over all the coast, perhaps backed by military force in its later stages. It was first detected by the replacement of local art styles on the coast by new ones which were influenced to a greater or less degree by that of Tiahuanaco, and this has since been supported by the discovery of changes in coastal building plans and burial customs. This is one of the main horizons, demonstrated by their art styles, to which reference has been made. The other, coming at the end of the Post-Classic Period and of aboriginal history, is the Inca horizon, which began its expansion in 1438 and finished with the Conquest. Between them was a period when Tiahuanaco influence was dying away, and local states, each with its own pottery style, were emerging in the north, central and south sections of the coast.

Similar chronological frameworks have been outlined for Mesoamerica and the Central Andes, and the dates attached to the various sub-divisions are not very different in the two areas, but it must be emphasized that there was little direct connexion between them, and that the word Classic is simply being used for a technological and artistic climax, without implying similar political conditions. The one period at which there is evidence for direct contact between the areas is at the beginning of the Chavín horizon about the ninth century B C, when the introduction of the jaguar cult and certain ceramic features point strongly to Mesoamerica, and particularly to Tlatilco in the Valley of Mexico. The route is uncertain, but it seems most likely at present that the contact was by sea. From this time onwards direct contacts ceased, and Peru followed its own lines of development.

In some respects it is difficult to compare the art of Peru with that of Mesoamerica, owing to differences in materials and in the degree of preservation. In architecture, many of the Peruvian sites which must have been most impressive are on the coast, where the usual building material is some form of adobe, or mud brick. Weathering may destroy the form of buildings in this material beyond recovery, whereas the stone buildings of Mesoamerica provide evidence, in their fallen stones, for reconstructions, many of which have been successfully carried out. Textiles, an outstanding feature of Peruvian art, are well preserved on the dry coast but are virtually non-existent in Mesoamerica. Metals, which did not appear in Mesoamerica until the Post-Classic Period, began to be used for ornaments something like 1,500 years earlier in Peru.

When all allowances have been made, Peruvian art as a whole does not rise to the levels reached by the chief Mesoamerican cultures. In craftsmanship it is unsurpassed, but it has the limitations of the craftsman's art, and as A. L. Kroeber said long ago, the craftsman's feet were mired down in technology and he felt with his hands rather than with his emotions. There is a marked difference between the two areas in the Post-Classic Period, when some elements of Peruvian art are singularly lacking in inspiration, in contrast to the vigour which is evident in Central Mexico until the end. This is particularly seen in the mould-made black pottery of the Chimú State on the north coast, where dullness and mass production go hand in hand. The quality of awe, which is so prominent in many Mesoamerican works of art, is most nearly approached in Peru in the stone carving of the Chavín horizon of the Formative Period, and this quality is present to some extent in the pottery and textiles of the Formative and Classic of the south coast, and the pottery and stone carving of the south highland Classic. The Classic of the north coast is distinguished for the realistic modelling and lively silhouette painting of the Mochica pottery, showing a competence and sureness of touch which is worthy of admiration. At all times some objects of great interest and considerable charm were produced, such as textiles, metal or inlaid work in wood, stone and shell.

PRECERAMIC PERIOD

When the first refuse deposit of the Preceramic Period was excavated in 1946 at the Huaca Prieta, at the mouth of the Chicama river on the north coast, the only finds which suggested the existence of any form of art were two small carved gourds in an extremely decayed condition. One of these gourds has four

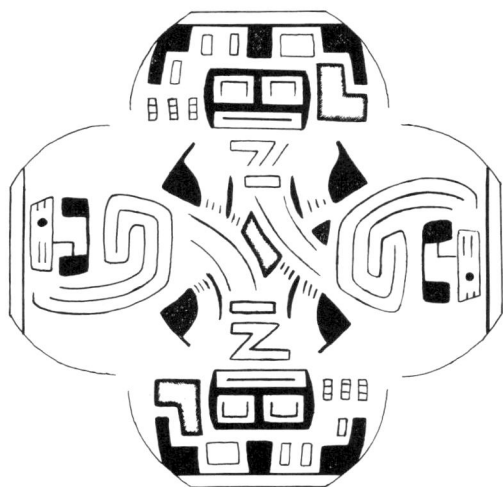

134, 135 Carved gourd vessel with cover found in an extremely fragile and decayed condition. *(left)* Drawing of the extended pattern seen on the gourd. Preceramic Period, *c.* 2000 B C. Huaca Prieta, Chicama Valley, North Coast.

highly schematic faces, skilfully and symmetrically placed, which can be regarded as some form of cat. The other bears what have been interpreted as two human figures interlocking across the bottom of the gourd, alternating with what look like two snakes in profile, and on the lid are two bird heads sharing a neck and forming a curvilinear Z-shaped figure *(Ills. 134, 135)*. They date from about 2000 B C. A great many plain gourds were found on this site, and it is remarkable that these were the only decorated ones. Carving, engraving and allied techniques are, indeed, very rare on any site at this period, and about the only examples which can be cited are a stone spindle whorl with a snake, a bird and a quadruped crudely engraved on it, and a bone pendant or spatula decorated by means of pricked dots with stars on one side and a pair of standing monkeys holding unidentified objects, perhaps blowpipes, on the other, both from Asia on the southern part of the coast.

To find anything related to the Huaca Prieta gourds, or indeed anything of any characteristic style, we must go to the textiles, of which there are more. The extremely fragmentary, decayed and faded condition of these has made their study very slow and difficult. They are distinguished from later ones by having been made exclusively by a variety of manual methods, without the aid of a heddle loom, and of these twining was that most frequently used. The fibres were spun cotton and a wild bast, probably milkweed. Colours were obtained by using natural white and brown cottons, by red, blue, yellow and orange dyes, and by rubbing dry red powder into the yarn, but none of these has been easy to detect. Feather work was made by knotting the ends of the feathers into half-hitch looped fabrics, and this must have provided brightly coloured garments but nothing is known of any pattern. There are a number of ingenious ways of producing patterns in twined fabrics, a highly characteristic one being based on warp transposition. The warps were set up in pairs of two different colours, for example each pair may consist of a red and a blue warp. By transposing these in opposite directions, say red to the right and blue to the left in one pick and back again in the next, a patch of red colour can be held to one face and one of blue to the other, and they can be reversed elsewhere in

136, 137 Fragment of twined cotton fabric *(left)* which had lost all traces of dy
The original design, a male condor with a snake in its stomach, was determined

the same fabric. In this sort of way, complicated designs were woven—distorted rectangular birds recognizable by their powerful hooked beaks, snakes with a head at each end, combined figures such as a double-headed snake with two rock crabs appended, and even a pair of fantastic human beings. The latter are associated with a pair of bird heads at either end of a common neck, a clear link with the gourd lid mentioned above. Where the colour has disappeared, as it generally has, the design has been recovered by noting the directions of displacement of the warps with the aid of a microscope and laboriously plotting them out *(Ills. 136, 137)*. Darning was used to a limited extent to produce plain weaves like those woven on a loom, but it is combined with twining in such a way as to exclude the possibility of using a heddle, and on cloths of this sort similar designs were made by means of warp floats. Designs were also made by forming holes of larger size than the normal in openwork looped fabrics, for instance a snake pattern found at Asia, and gauze appears to have been used elsewhere to produce interlocking fish heads. Although these designs are based on nature, the idea of combining two creatures, the double heads, and the way in which they are shown are highly sophisticated.

the analysis of every yarn movement. The photograph could thus be retouched to show how the piece originally looked *(right)*. Preceramic Period. Chicama Valley

It is true that the limitations of textile techniques must have imposed the general angularity of the designs, as they did right through Peruvian prehistory, but this is not all. The makers of these textiles were preceded by people who lacked cotton but buried their dead wrapped in twined rush mats, so the main technique was there, but at some time they began to apply it in very ingenious ways to the depiction in strange fashions of themselves and some of the creatures they saw around them. Where the stimulus came from we do not know, and the rarity of suitable conditions for preservation may mean that we shall never know. Twining as a way of making textiles ceased with the arrival of the heddle loom about 1200 B C, but double-headed, angular, interlocking creatures persisted until the Spaniards brought the ancient civilizations of Peru to an end.

Until recently, nothing was known of art in the highlands before Chavín, but a series of pre-Chavín stages is now known from Kotosh on the Huallaga river. The earliest, before 1800 B C, which appears to be Preceramic, has a rectangular stone temple on a high platform, adorned inside with plaster reliefs showing crossed hands.

THE CHAVIN HORIZON

The next episode in the art of the coast was the appearance of the Chavín horizon in the ninth century, but in the highlands decorated grey pottery appeared about 1800 B C at Kotosh. This has incised geometrical designs, painted after firing with red and rarely yellow and white. Chavínoid features appeared about 1000 B C, accompanied by some remarkable red pottery with broad-line incised designs which include human faces, painted on it with graphite after firing. Pure Chavín pottery is found shortly after. Chavín itself is an important temple some 10,000 feet up on the eastern slope of the Andes, in a small valley which ultimately flows into the Marañón, and it lies east of that upper part of the Santa Valley called the Callejón de Huaylas. Although it is not necessarily the centre of the style in Peru, its importance is unquestionable. Other highland sites are known but little inform-

138 Annular vessel of yellowish-grey ware with
stirrup spout. On the rim are two human
heads and two heads combining bird (probably owl) and feline features. Late Cupisnique (Coast Chavin) style. North Coast

139 Upper part of the Great Image, a monolith
of white granite representing a human figure
with feline fangs and snakes as hair. Double
feline faces sharing a single jaw are shown
on the projection above the head and elsewhere on the figure. Probably ninth century
B C. From the oldest part of the temple at
Chavín de Huántar

140 Part of symmetrical frieze of birds decorated with feline jaws and eyes, and snake heads. Lintel of the black and white portal in the temple at Chavín de Huántar

ation about them is available. Sites of the same period are found in coastal valleys, namely Cerro Sechín and Moxeke in the Casma Valley, and Punkurí and Cerro Blanco in the Nepeña Valley. There are rather close stylistic links between Chavín and Cerro Blanco, Moxeke and Punkurí are linked to one another and to Chavín, but Sechín is peculiar although it has features which connect it with Moxeke. The Chavín style is expressed chiefly by a notable pottery type at other coastal sites in the north *(Ills. 145, 146, 147)*, and its influence is seen in the southern coastal pottery style of Paracas, and in textiles from the central and south coast. The Chavín style is marked architecturally by massive terraced pyramidal platforms, of stone at Chavín itself, and of conical adobes or rubble set in mud mortar on the coast. Chavín art has recently been the subject of an important study by J. H. Rowe, and frequent reference will be made to it.

At Chavín itself, Rowe has distinguished several building stages, all similarly faced with regular courses of stone slabs, some of them thicker than the others. The interior is traversed by a connected series of galleries and chambers on two or three levels, efficiently ventilated by means of stone shafts. A row of human and feline heads was tenoned into the outside wall, and higher up was a projecting cornice of squared slabs with carvings on the under side and in some cases on the outer side also. The oldest part is a U-shaped block, open to the east, in the depths of which, in a dark passage, is what is called the *Lanzón* or the Great Image *(Ill. 139)*, nearly 15 feet high, of white granite, roughly prismatic in shape with a thinner projection at the top, carved in low relief to form a human figure with feline fangs. Rowe says that it has, in its setting, 'an awe-inspiring quality which can be felt even by a present-

146

day unbeliever'. Additions were made on either side of this block of buildings, and later on the south side alone, thus forming a great rectangular mass and changing the centre of gravity of the plan, a change which coincided, it is suggested, with a transfer of worship to a new image within it which can no longer be found. Access to the new southern block is through a portal, the north half of black limestone and the south of white granite, the doorway being flanked by a pair of grey andesite columns supporting a lintel on top of which was a striking frieze of standing birds, much of which still exists (Ill. 140). Each column bears a composite figure in flat relief, having a human body and bird head, wings and claws, all liberally decorated with feline eyes and fangs. In front of the entrance is a sunken court flanked by buildings.

Other carvings at Chavín come from the cornice slabs, of which a notable example shows a jaguar, whose tail emerges from a fanged face and whose body is sprinkled with eyes, while snake heads sprout from the margin. Another slab shows a standing figure with cat face and hair composed of snakes, holding a conch and a spondylus shell in his hands, another shows a bat, and another a bird with a staring feline face on its body. Rowe suggests that, since these exterior carvings were part of the architectural decoration, they were not themselves objects of worship, though they may in some cases depict supernatural beings. On the other hand, there are two carvings which, like the Great Image, are more likely from their form and careful finish to have been cult objects. One is a long rectangular shaft called the Tello obelisk (after its discoverer, the Peruvian archaeologist Dr Tello), which bears carved alligators accompanied by lesser beings and decorated with the usual eyes and fangs. The other is the famous Raimondi stela now

in Lima, a great rectangular slab over 6 feet high, showing a standing figure with feline face and claws, holding a staff in each hand,
crowned with a great superstructure consisting of a series of
grotesque upward-looking faces armed with fangs and surrounded
by an aureole of snakes and scrolls. Rowe has suggested that this
was a visible representation of the god hidden and worshipped in
the newer southern block of the temple.

The commonest Chavín carvings are birds, which Rowe gives
reasons to identify as eagles and hawks, not the condors they have
generally been called, whereas cats (mainly jaguars) are less
frequent, but almost all, whether birds, cats or others, are immen-
sely complicated by the addition of what at first sight appear to
be decorative features, especially feline fangs or faces, eyes or
snake heads. It is clear that they are more than this and Rowe
has suggested that they were supposed to have definite meanings,
the feline features for instance indicating divinity and the snakes,
hair. Whether this is accepted or not, the almost universal presence
of jaguar attributes points to the importance of his cult.

Much Chavín carving is in flat relief, in which details are shown
on flat surfaces by engraving or by cutting away the background,
in fact a sort of champlevé, but the tenoned heads show that carving in the round was also practised, as do the small objects like
mortars found at various sites. Other features of the style are
a tendency to bilateral symmetry and to repetition, both of which
can be illustrated by the bands of faces with feline jaws on the
projection above the head of the Great Image and on its belt.
These, although in profile, have an eye and a nostril on either
side of the mouth, which is thus shared by two faces. There is
also a tendency to reduce anatomical features to straight lines and
simple curves, and to subordinate the drawing of a figure to a
framework of straight bands as though following ruled guide-lines.
Zig-zag bands within a frame representing jaws with teeth, and a
multitude of fangs may be carved in what appears to be rather an
aimless fashion on bodies or wings, as on the figures decorating
the columns of the black and white portal, and these and the sharp
points formed when two curves meet give a prickly appearance

141 Low relief carving of bird decorated with feline heads in profile. Just below the damaged bird head are two feline faces sharing one jaw. Temple at Chavín de Huántar

to the surface of many Chavín reliefs. There is a general effect of massive angularity about Chavín carvings, which becomes more marked after the earliest stage, and this may be due in part to the influence of textile patterns which have not survived.

The Chavín style must have lasted a considerable time, perhaps about 500 years. Comparisons with the Paracas pottery style in the south show that its influence in that quarter had faded by about 300 B C. In the north, its influence was inherited by the much later Mochica pottery, and it may in remote areas have overlapped that style to some extent, but it is unlikely that the Chavínoid ceremonial centres survived much longer than the influence in the south of the style associated with them. During the life of the style, there were changes in detail, and Rowe has worked out a succession. It must suffice here to say that the Great Image in the oldest part of the Chavín temple appears to be one of the earliest carvings, and the Raimondi stela one of the latest, with the Tello obelisk followed by the carvings surrounding the black and white portal occupying intermediate positions.

Turning to the coastal sites, Cerro Blanco in the Nepeña Valley has not been very fully described, but it certainly includes courts on different levels enclosed by low rubble walls faced with clay plaster, modelled in pure Chavín style to show faces, eyes and fangs, painted brickred and greenish-yellow. It is possible that some jaguar masks in an imperfect state are made up of a pair of profile bird masks, and it has been suggested that the whole complex was meant to represent a bird in plan. Punkurí, in the same valley, is a terraced platform with a stairway on which stands a bizarre jaguar head and front paws, modelled in the round from mud and rubble and painted, with the grave of a sacrificed woman at its feet. Higher up the structure are walls of conical adobes, plastered with clay and decorated with incised designs of Chavín character, which Tello, the discoverer, considered to belong to a slightly later building stage. Of the sites in the Casma Valley, Moxeke is a terraced platform or pyramid which appears to have been partly faced with a mosaic of irregular stones. The upper part is much destroyed, but there appear to have been two high platforms side by side, rising from the back of a broad terrace which was partly occupied by a slightly sunken court, a feature which has been noted at other sites of the same age. Moxeke is known chiefly for a remarkable series of four clay plastered demi-figures and two heads, made of conical adobes, mud and stones, modelled in the round and painted black, white, red, blue and green, standing in niches separated by sections bearing figures in low relief. All are much damaged, but the best two of the demi-figures wear a sort of pleated kilt and a short cape, one of which is adorned with pendants in the form of four snakes almost identical with the stone ones of Chavín. Cerro Sechín was a temple of complex plan on a raised platform, but it is chiefly remarkable for what seems to have been the retaining wall of the platform, on either side of the stairway. It is composed of upright flat stones of irregular outline, alternating with smaller stones set above one another in pairs or threes. All bear strange incised designs, those on the uprights mostly standing men wearing loin cloths and truncated conical hats and carrying staves or clubs, but some appear to be conquered enemies because they lack weapons and have a limp appearance, while one appears to have been cut in half and one is a corpse without legs (*Ill. 142*). This group sometimes has the sort of pleated kilt seen on the

142 Two engraved slabs. A human figure with severed legs *(left)*, and a trophy head *(right)*. Chavín Period. Part of retaining wall of temple platform at Cerro Sechín, Casma Valley

Moxeke figures, and this forms a link with them. Apart from the figures, one upright has six pairs of faces piled up on top of one another, and some are non-representational. The smaller stones have severed heads in profile, the earliest known example of the head-hunter's trophy in Peruvian art. The style of the carvings as a whole is quite unlike that of Chavín, but in addition to the link with Moxeke already mentioned some small objects from various parts of the coast bear designs which are common to the two styles. The dissimilarity is probably partly due to age differences, and writers have disagreed as to which is the older, but Collier and Thompson, who have worked most recently in Casma, regard Moxeke and Cerro Sechín as derivative from Chavín rather than as its prototype, though the stage at Chavín to which the influence belongs is not yet known. Resemblances have been claimed to exist between the men on the stones at Cerro Sechín and the

143 Circular gold, repoussé plaque. Feline face with snake head appendages, within guilloche border. Late Chavín style. Possibly from Chavín de Huántar

Danzantes (Ill. 13) at Monte Albán in Oaxaca, Mexico, but it is doubtful if this amounts to more than that both are incised figures on flat stones.

Among the smaller stone carvings of Chavín style are mortars, bowls, plates and mace-heads. Prominent among these is a mortar in the form of a jaguar *(Ill. 144)*, probably from Chavín, now in the University Museum at Philadelphia, which Rowe ascribes to the earliest stage of the Chavín style. In spite of its comparatively small size—it is 13 inches long—it gives an impression of massive strength appropriate to a much larger object. Its jaguar markings have been stylized into L shapes and crosses. Two other animal mortars, from Pacopampa, the northernmost of the known Chavín sites, both show feline fangs, but one of them has a beak also, and this has been taken to show a combination of feline and owl. The other has the upper lip split in the middle, and from each half of it rises a volute enclosing the nostril. Both mortars have pestles with a feline head at the end of the handle, and both have the nostrils shown by the same convention as that of the second mortar, which is worth mentioning because a similar figure is transferred to form a sort of eyebrow on feline owl heads on a pot which will be described later. The under side of a plate from the north coast shows a relief carving of a quadruped with two feline heads, a combination of the Chavín feline with the Preceramic heritage of two-headed figures. A cylindrical vessel in the Bliss Collection shows two grotesque dancing figures connected by a scroll or rope, each of them with a prolonged dentate jaw band with two pairs of fangs and one at the end. Many examples of the same sort could be given, in bone and shell as well as stone. The mace heads are graceful and doubtless effective objects with projecting flanges and points.

Gold, worked by hammering, welding and soldering, first appears on the Chavín horizon. Examples are a repoussé standing figure with fanged mouth holding two staves on a rectangular plaque, and another on a cylindrical crown, both from the Lambayeque Valley. Ear-spools with snake head and bird head designs are known from the same area, and in the Bliss Collection is a

144 Mortar in the shape of a jaguar, with stylized markings. Stone carved in the round and incised. The eyes were originally inlaid. Chavín Culture

circular plaque, possibly from Chavín, with a feline face with snake
head appendages in the middle, surrounded by a guilloche whose
angularity betokens a late stage in the style *(Ill. 143)*.

The Chavín pottery of the coast is named Cupisnique, after the
valley where it was first found. Typically it is a hard, monochrome
ware, black, grey or buff in colour, decorated by modelling, incision, or some way of roughening the surface such as punctation
or rocker stamping *(Ill. 145)*, a feature already seen at Tlatilco in
Mexico (see page 32).   There is only a limited amount of painting,
chiefly in black and red, confined to the latter part of the period.
The most typical shape is a closed vessel with a flat base and a
stirrup spout, which consists of an arched tube with the spout
emerging from the highest point *(Ill. 146)*.   The stirrup spout
is a form which is found on the north coast, with some interruptions,
until the end of Pre-Columbian times, and these early examples are
typically heavy in outline, with a relatively small opening under the
stirrup and a low concave-sided spout, though some lighter forms
are present and may be ascribed to the later stages. (Some which

154

146 Stirrup-spouted early Cupisnique jar of dark monochrome pottery, with rough surface perhaps suggested by a spondylus shell

have been claimed as Cupisnique, largely on grounds of colour, may belong to the later Mochica Culture.) Another common form is a jar with a narrow concave-sided neck, the upper part of which resembles the top of the stirrup spout. The bodies of these vessels may be spheroidal apart from the flat base, and decorated by incision with designs which in many cases include feline faces or fangs, and these may be emphasized by covering the background with punctation or rocker stamping. More typical are forms modelled in the round or in high relief to represent a wide variety of subjects, such as animal or human forms, houses, mollusc shells and vegetables. One remarkable vessel shows a nursing mother (*Ill. 147*), one an aged wrinkled face, and a third is a hollow ring bearing two human heads and two heads which are combined feline and bird, probably owl (*Ill. 138*). One feline owl has open eyes and the other has stylized ones in Chavín style, and one human face has open eyes and the other closed ones, possibly meant to show a contrast in each case between life and death. This is the vessel on which the double volutes into which the nostrils developed on the stone pestles and mortars have been moved up to form a sort of eyebrow on the feline owl faces. These pots are the earliest examples of the north coast tradition of realistic modelling, which reached its climax in the Classic Mochica Culture and was revived in an inferior form in the Post-Classic Chimú.

On the central coast, objects of pottery, wood and bone in Chavín style have been reported from a cemetery at Ancón, and three very curious instances of bird-feline heads, showing both beaks and fangs, in patches of cotton tapestry forming part of a loosely-woven plain weave cloth, were found in Professor Willey's excavations at Supe in the same area.

Far to the south in the Nasca and Ica valleys are graves belonging to the Paracas stage of the middle and later Formative. The early stages of this were deeply influenced by Chavín, and this is seen not only in incised and resin-painted depictions of fanged feline jaws on jars of local shapes but also in feline faces with extra

147 Modelled stirrup-spouted Cupisnique jar of dark pottery, representing a woman suckling her child

fangs and snake head appendages in pure Chavín style on painted cotton cloths. As has been said already, direct Chavín influence on the art of this area faded by about 300 B C, giving place to local developments.

The Later Formative and Classic Periods
After the Chavín horizon, different traditions developed in various parts of the country, and existing differences were accentuated. The main known areas of importance at this time are the north coast, the north ,highlands, the south coast and the south highlands. Artistically the central coast was unimportant, and the central highlands are virtually unknown.

THE NORTH COAST
During the later centuries B C the pure Chavín tradition died away, and a decorated pottery style of rather a different character called Salinar is found in graves in the Chicama Valley and to a lesser extent in the Virú Valley just to the south. This is its general position, but it is not clear to what extent it overlapped its predecessor and its successor. It was not accompanied by other artistic features of note.

It is distinguished by oxidized firing which produced red and brown colours, and sometimes has simple decoration such as lines, dots, triangles and steps in thin white paint. Vessel forms include (i) a modified form of stirrup-spouted jar, (ii) a spout and bridge jar in which a sloping spout was balanced by a figure, head or some other object, and joined to it by a thin bridge handle, and (iii) a bottle with a narrow vertical neck and loop handle. The first and third may be modelled or carry a modelled figure on the top, but the modelling is less accomplished than that of Cupisnique, though sometimes more lively (*Ill. 148*). Among the modelled forms are birds, animals, heads, houses, and little naked human beings or pairs of them which may be in erotic attitudes. The first Peruvian whistling jars are found among the spout and bridge forms, in which the figure is shown blowing a spherical whistle, which will sound when water is put into the jar and swung to and fro. In

157

later styles the whistle is hidden inside the figure. The style as a whole may show influence from the south, since the spout and bridge is essentially a south coast form, and white-on-red decoration may originate from the central coast. It is sometimes regarded as representing a white-on-red horizon of rather limited distribution.

A pottery style particularly characteristic of the Virú Valley, which is thought to begin after Salinar and to persist while the early stages of the Classic Mochica developed in the Chicama Valley, is called Virú or Gallinazo *(Ills. 149, 150)*. It includes stirrup spouts, spout and bridge pots with single or double containers, and wide-mouthed jars, with modelling if anything less realistic than that of Salinar, but its chief characteristic is negative or resist painting, in which designs in the colour of the vessel, generally red, appear against a black background. This is done by covering the areas to remain free of black with a resist such as wax or clay after firing.

149 Red spout and bridge jar with simple linear negative painting in black. Virú or Gallinazo style. Late Formative or Early Classic. Probably from Virú Valley

150 Spout and bridge jar representing a warrior carrying club and shield on a reed raft, with negative painting. Virú or Gallinazo style. Early Classic

The vessel is then smoked, or dipped in black stain and perhaps heated to fix it, after which the resist is removed. In the central and north coast this style follows the white-on-red and a negative horizon has been postulated on the strength of it, but when a larger area is considered it appears that this form of decoration started in this region on the south coast and spread northwards, reaching the north highlands in the Classic Period.

There is little to say about architecture in the northern valleys at this stage. Large terraced pyramids were built in Virú in the Gallinazo Period, using rectangular adobes marked by the cane moulds in which they were made, and some structures of this kind were built on steep spurs commanding the valley and were associated with platforms and rooms, all enclosed within a rock wall. These fortified sanctuaries derive a certain grandeur from their situation even in their decay. At a site on the valley floor a sunken court associated with such a pyramid had a retaining wall with two horizontal bands of geometrical decoration made by setting a row of mould-made adobe blocks with inset crosses above a row in the form of steps, with the background deeply recessed in each case. These blocks were painted green, red and yellow, with the recesses black, and the rest of the wall was white.

The Classic Period is marked by the development of the Mochica Culture, which originated in the Chicama and Moche Valleys and later spread south by conquest of the Virú Valley and beyond. It is distinguished by its well-known funerary pottery, of which the stirrup spout is the commonest form, but there are many others, including bell-shaped bowls with ring bases, flasks with flaring collars, double whistling jars and approximately hemispherical bowls. There are three forms of decoration—modelling in the round, modelling in low relief, and painting. The first is a continuation, and the acme, of the realistic modelling tradition of the area, but is more closely related to the Cupisnique variety than to Salinar or Gallinazo. Unlike Mexico, Peru has comparatively few figurines in comparison with its modelled pots at this period, or at any other time. A great deal of stress has been laid on Mochica realism, but it is only realistic within limits, and

151 Pottery bowl with fish alternating with decorative panels. With pressed relief, painted in red and white. Mochica

what the potters did was to stress a salient feature, such as the head of a figure with an elaborate head-dress, which they would represent with great fidelity, so catching the observer's attention that he does not notice that they have paid little attention to some other parts such as the lower limbs. Many modelled pots were made in moulds, themselves of pottery, and the same applies to those decorated in low relief, generally called pressed relief *(Ill. 151)*, but minor differences are introduced during the finishing process, so exact replicas are less frequent than might be expected. Most of the pots are painted in white and red, and the introduction of a little black and orange is a sign of a late stage in the period. This restraint in colour is characteristic of the north coast, and not only at this period. Some vessels lack modelled decoration and are skilfully painted with a wide variety of subjects in profile, including elaborate scenes, in red on a white ground *(Ill. 154)*. Unlike the modelled figures which appear static, many of them are designed to give an effect of movement which is accentuated in the later

stages, particularly when elaborately dressed figures appear to chase one another round a pot. The various modes of decoration are not mutually exclusive, and an example may be quoted which has a deer resting on the top of the pot and a deer hunt painted on the body (*Ill. 155*). Five chronological stages, based on changes in the form of the stirrup spout and the nature of the decoration, have been distinguished, but the pottery is thin and well made throughout the period. Early Mochica stirrup spouts have much in common with Cupisnique ones (*Ills. 146,147*), but stirrups later become larger, lighter and finally somewhat angular, and the spout loses its rim, becomes longer, passes through a tendency to have concave sides and many develop a slight taper. Painted scenes are introduced in the middle stages, and later become more complex and restless.

The subjects of the decoration on Mochica pots are extremely varied, and give valuable information about the life of the people. Plants, animals and birds are shown, and in some cases the species can be identified. There are naked prisoners, people with amputated

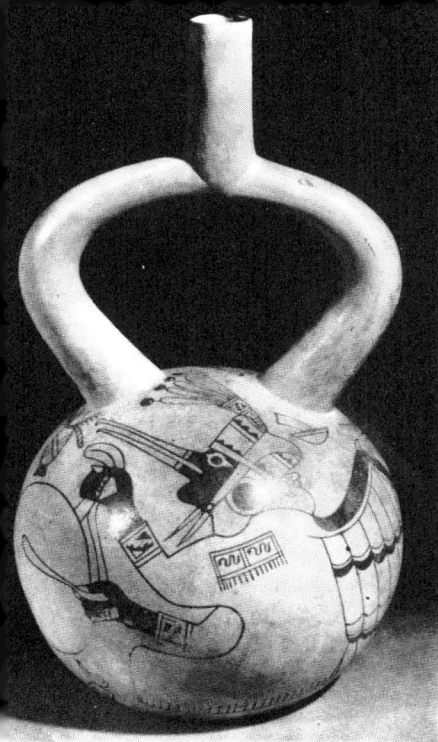

152-155 Four stirrup-spouted Mochica vessels. The first *(opposite left)* in the form of a house, painted in red and white. The second *(opposite right)* in the form of a seated man. Incised and scraped, highly polished red slip. Early Mochica. The third *(above left)*, painted in red and white, shows a drummer wearing a humming bird mask and wings. Late Mochica. The fourth *(above right)* is decorated with a warrior chasing a spotted deer. A three-dimensional figure of a deer tops the vessel. Modelled and painted in red and white

156 Bone spatula handle with the engraved figure of a warrior dressed as a bird, and inset turquoise and pyrite nodules. Mochica. Santa Valley

157 Wooden head, inlaid with shell and turquoise, of a ceremonial digging stick. It shows a tusked figure holding a digging stick and accompanied by a boy. Mochica. Found in the grave of an old man and boy similarly dressed, at Huaca de la Cruz, Virú Valley

limbs or identifiable diseases, warriors, weapons, buildings *(Ill. 152)*, enthroned rulers, portraits *(Ills. 158, 159)* and gods. The well-known erotic scenes form but a small proportion of the whole (a figure of 2% has been quoted). Painting and pressed relief include such diverse subjects as a procession of skeletons playing pan-pipes and a textile workshop. All bear witness to a complex, specialized, theocratic society, in which fighting played an important part.

Monumental architecture shows little that is new. It may be exemplified by the two enormous terraced pyramidal masses of unbonded adobes which make up the pyramids of the Sun and Moon in the Moche Valley between Virú and Chicama. Although they are rarely preserved, parts of buildings of this age were adorned with wall paintings of much the same character as the vase paintings, but without the colour restriction, as many as seven (black, white, red, grey, yellow, brown and blue) being noted on one example. The subjects were outlined by incision on the plaster, and patches of colour then painted in. A famous example at Moche showed personified weapons in battle with human beings, and getting the best of it. Another, discovered a few years ago at Pañamarca in the Nepeña Valley, shows a procession taking prisoners to sacrifice, illustrating a characteristic of this sort of painting, that the importance of a person was in proportion to his size.

Sculpture on a large scale is virtually unknown, but small objects were carved in various materials such as stone, bone *(Ill. 156)*, wood and shell. A good example is the contents of the grave of an old warrior priest of late Mochica date found in the Virú Valley. Among many other things, this contained three wooden staves. One of them is a copper-shod ceremonial digging stick, at the top of which is carved, and decorated with multi-coloured shell inlay, the figure of a tusked god (carrying his own digging stick), whom the old man himself was accoutred to impersonate *(Ill. 157)*. The second was an old war-club, with a pear-shaped head carved with a battle scene in low relief. The third was surmounted by an owl. Such carvings in general have much in common with the pottery modelling; they share its limited realism, and they gain interest from inlays of shell or turquoise.

158 Mochica portrait vase, a particularly fine example, painted in white and red

159 Mochica portrait vase with stirrup spout of a man wearing a decorated cap painted in red and white

Metalwork was well developed at this time, and gold, silver, copper and their alloys were worked and used for ornaments thoughout the coast. The north coast was exceptional in using copper for tools and weapons as well, and furnishes the best examples of metalwork in general. Particularly pleasing are small and delicate Mochica objects in which gold is combined with other materials, such as a pair of ear ornaments in the form of mosaic discs representing warriors in turquoise, shell and gold framed by a circular beaded gold rim, or a lunate nose-ornament of turquoise with a small gold mask in the middle and fringed with turquoise beads. A magnificent and unique object of unknown use, in the Mugica Gallo Collection, is a sheet-gold puma skin with the hollow head ingeniously modelled in the round. The body is made of two thicknesses of gold, each with a different form of repoussé decoration (*Ill. 160*).

Remains which have been found in this area are enough to show a wide range of textile techniques, but they are rarely well preserved, and it is better to speak of this art in connexion with the south coast, where it was outstanding.

THE NORTH HIGHLANDS

Less is known about the north highlands than about the coast, but the chief artistic developments are found in two areas.

The first of these is the upper part of the Santa Valley and its environs, known as the Callejón de Huaylas. Here arose a notable pottery style called Recuay, which is thought to have developed out of a variety of the negative painted style of Virú found in the lower reaches of the Santa Valley itself. It flourished during Classic times. The vessels are of many shapes, very typical being flat-based globular jars with a constricted neck which may open out sharply into a wide flange round the mouth, or flare out gently. Most have some modelling on the body, generally in the form of a head, which may have a subsidiary tube spout emerging sideways from the mouth or the head-dress (*Ill. 161*). Some more elaborate forms have the neck rising from one side of the body, the top of which is flattened to form a step where a group of modelled

160 Gold puma skin with three-dimensional head. On the animal's tongue a human ▶ face appears, and on its body a design of double two-headed serpents. The belly in two thicknesses forms a pouch. Gold repoussé work and wire. Mochica

161 Jar with flange mouth and lateral spout emerging above a modelled human head between two animals. Decorated with black negative painting over white and red, showing a crested jaguar and other features. Recuay style. Callejón de Huaylas, North Highlands

figures may stand. Among forms of which several varieties are known is a modelled one showing a man leading a llama. Highly characteristic of Recuay pottery is black negative painting over a red and white ground, and many vessels have one or more examples of a jaguar with a large crest in this technique, and also steps, circles or dots. Ideas travelled between here and the Mochica area, and the modelling shows Mochica influence though it is far stiffer and more stylized. In the other direction is the rare occurrence of the flange mouth and lateral spout on Mochica jars.

No notable buildings have been ascribed to the Classic period in the Callejón, and the pottery comes from stone-lined subterranean galleries and box-like graves. Numbers of stone statues have been found; they are a metre or less high, of pillar-like or roughly conical form, showing no competence in carving in the round but a certain amount of ability in indicating surface detail. The brows and nose are shown as a T-shaped figure, the eyes are round and in relief, and the neck is hollowed out to throw the pointed chin into relief, but the other detail is very shallow. Squatting women and warriors can be distinguished among the subjects, the latter having decorated shields and wearing head trophies. There are also slabs showing felines and men in low relief, and these have features which link them to the statues and to Recuay pottery. The stone work does not approach its Chavín predecessors in quality.

The second highland area is round Cajamarca. Here an independent pottery style developed through later Formative and Classic times *(Ill. 162)*. It is called Cursive, from its lightly painted running scroll-like designs in brownish black or red on a white or cream ground. Small, highly stylized animals or heads may appear among the cursive scrolls, which are mostly found on the interiors of open bowls on low ring bases.

162 Bowl and two sherds, painted with cursive scroll pattern, including stylized faces and animals. Colours vary from red-brown to black, with some grey on the bowl, on a cream ground. Cajamarca, North Highlands

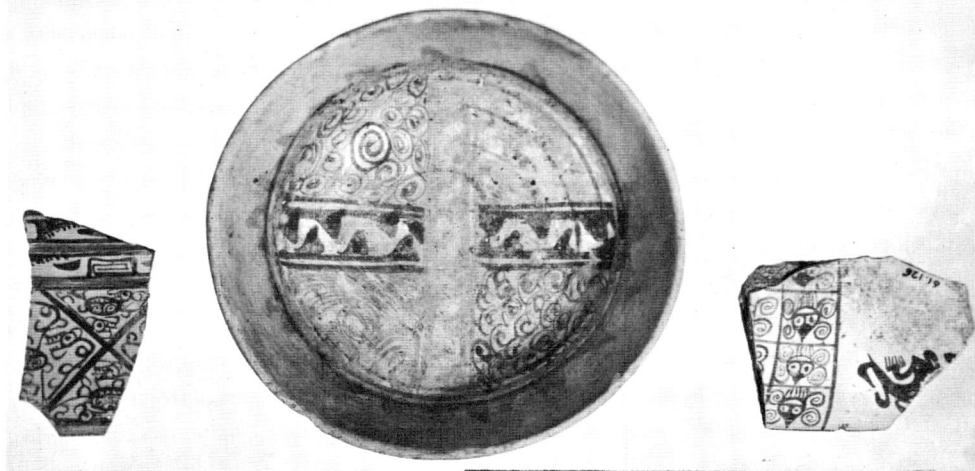

THE CENTRAL COAST

This area is of less artistic interest than its neighbours, although it contains prominent ceremonial centres in the form of clusters of pyramidal platforms built of rectangular adobes. Maranga, near Lima, is an example, and the earliest ruins of the important shrine of Pachacámac in the Lurín Valley are another. Here is a platform of many low terraces, each about 3 feet high, with polychrome paintings of plants and animals, surrounded by many later buildings.

The Classic pottery style of the area is called Interlocking, from the way in which angular designs derived from textile patterns interlock with one another. They are painted in rather dingy black, white and red colours on simple vessels such as bowls, beakers and jars, and the commonest of them are snakes and fish, or their heads.

THE SOUTH COAST

The earliest known Formative stage of any artistic significance is estimated to be rather later than the beginning of Chavín, and it gave rise to a different tradition, which we know largely from the very prominent cult of the dead. A large number of rich burials have been found; they are in a crouched position, unlike those of the north which are generally extended. One type, found in groups in deep, dome-shaped, rock-cut tombs, includes many individuals with skulls which have been trepanned, in some cases repeatedly, and another type, found in large numbers in rectangular pits, have highly deformed skulls. They are wrapped in many layers of specially-made textiles in mint condition, the making of which must have occupied many workers for a prodigious amount of time and involved far more effort than the grave deposits of the north, the chief constituent of which is pottery.

In pottery the south coast tradition is expressed by successive phases in the Formative Paracas style and the Classic Nasca style, upon which the chronological succession is based. It is distinguished by emphasis on colour, as many as eight colours appearing on some Classic pots, with no great skill in representational model-

163 Dark grey-brown spout and bridge vessel, the spout balanced by a stylized bird's head. The surface is burnished except for the bird's head and a large feline face incised at one end, some details of which are picked out in red paint applied after firing. Paracas style, Formative Period. South Coast

ling *(Ill. 165)*, as against the naturalistic modelling and restraint in colour of the north, and such life forms as are painted on pots are highly stylized. There is no interest in the realistic depiction of people and scenes in everyday surroundings, but rather in macabre features such as fantastic demons and a profusion of severed human heads, which is in accord with the exaggerated interest shown in the dead. Vessels have rounded bases, open bowls are very common, and the jar with spouts connected by a bridge, in which one spout may be replaced by a bird or human head, takes the place of the stirrup spout of the north. Beakers became common in the Nasca style *(Ill. 168)*.

Paracas pottery is decorated by incision, which may outline designs in vivid resinous colours painted after firing *(Ill. 164)*. The colours of these paints include red, yellow, orange, white, dark blue, dark green, black and brown, and are characteristic of the Paracas stage. The designs are feline faces *(Ill. 163)*, guilloches or geometrical forms such as circles or steps. Negative decoration,

164 Buff double spout and bridge vessel, with incised decoration suggesting matting on body and bridge. Parts of this are picked out in red, yellow, black and white resinous paint applied after firing. Paracas style, Formative Period. South Coast

consisting mainly of dots on a smudged background, was also used, and together they were the first experimental attempts at pottery decoration in the area. The earliest known Paracas phase is thought have begun about 700 BC, and was strongly influenced by the Chavín style, an influence seen particularly in the feline faces. By about 300 BC the direct Chavín influence had died away and a local style prevailed, even in feline designs *(Ill. 166)*. There were minor changes in existing forms and new ones, including doll-like effigy jars, were introduced, as was a new form of decoration consisting of fine line designs produced by burnishing on black ware. Finally, in what is called the Early or Proto-Nasca stage, about AD 100, the resinous colours were replaced by normal pigments applied before firing, while the incised outlines were retained. The dropping of the incision, perhaps a century later, is held to mark the beginning of the Classic Nasca style.

165 Spout and bridge effigy jar modelled to represent a woman, and painted in black, white, dark red, yellow and orange. Nasca style, Classic Period. South Coast

166 Burnished black spout and bridge vessel representing a jaguar. The markings are incised, and most of the surface was probably originally covered with resinous post-fired colours, of which some red, yellow, grey and white remain. Paracas style, Formative Period. South Coast

167 Double spout and bridge vessel decorated with two rows of crabs. Red, orange, and dark grey paint over dark red slip. Early Nasca, Classic Period

Classic Nasca can be divided into many stages, but it is convenient to group them into two main ones. In the first of these, the background slip is either a sombre red or white, and in the second it is generally white. Over these the designs are painted in three to eight colours, of which shades of red, black, white, brown, yellow, grey and violet are the most usual. The designs fall into two main groups, the first consisting of recognizable but stylized birds, fish *(Ill. 167)* or plants and the second of religious or mythological themes, such as the demons or trophy heads already mentioned, which become more frequent in the later stages at the expense of the first group. In the first stage the designs are fairly compact, whereas later they become more florid and tend to sprawl all over the background. Rowe has recently pointed out that the more recognizable natural forms come in the middle of the Paracas-Nasca sequence as a whole, early in Classic Nasca, with the more extravagant and stylized forms before and after. This is contrary to the common assumption, on which the original seriation of the Nasca style was based, that natural forms invariably come earliest in such a sequence. Within the limited range to

168 Beaker painted in red, purplish red, grey, yellow and black on a white ground, showing a demon between inner bands of geometrical design and outer ones of trophy heads. Late Nasca, Classic Period. South Coast

which it was applied, this seriation gave the right results, but it need not have done so.

The other great artistic medium in the south was textile production, and this is not due merely to better conditions of preservation than those in the north. Early in the Paracas succession such normal weaving techniques as gauze, brocade and double cloth in combinations of alpaca wool and cotton were in use, but the most notable feature of the phase is embroidery. This became fashionable later and persisted to some extent into the Nasca phase, but was used very little afterwards. The finest examples have come from the mummy bundles in the rectangular graves at Paracas, and consist of mantles, shirts, loin-cloths, turbans and other garments, embroidered in vivid reds, blues, yellows, greens, browns and other colours, all derived from combinations of red, yellow and indigo dyes with the colours of the natural cotton and wool. The designs include grotesque winged and masked humans, combined human and animal monsters holding trophy heads, animals, fish and birds, with little attempt at naturalism. Individual figures are small in scale, but they may be

169 (*left*) Part of the border of a mantle, covered with solid alpaca wool embroidery, showing outlines of small cats within larger ones, in rose red, yellow and dark blue. Paracas

170 (*below*) Rare type of tapestry in rose pink, light blue and yellow with a design showing a stylized monster worked in small shell beads strung on the warp. Nasca

171 Lay figure dressed in richly embroidered mantle, turban and undergarments, from a Paracas mummy

powdered over the surface of a garment in different colour combinations with gorgeous effect. Complete garments survive, and the figures dressed in them in the National Museum at Lima are a splendid sight *(Ill. 171)*. Other noteworthy techniques were designs formed by plain weave against a background of gauze, and painting on cloth showing a much surer touch than later examples.

There are two strains in Paracas textile design, a curvilinear and a rectilinear one, which seem to reflect the passage of time to some extent. None but rectilinear designs are found in the early stages, and they were encouraged by the use of true textile techniques. A tendency to outline them gives a transparent effect, which may be accentuated by outline figures in a contrasting colour inside them, for example birds or miniature cats may be shown within large cats *(Ill. 169)*. Embroidery encouraged curvilinear designs built up in solid patches of colour, although rectilinear ones were far from being excluded, and there was a tendency at later stages towards floridity and the development of appendages and space-fillers, recalling the evolution of painting on Nasca pots. With the coming of Classic Nasca, tapestry and other textile techniques increased *(Ill. 170)* and embroidery diminished in importance.

About architecture there is little to say. As in other areas, ceremonial centres were based on stepped pyramids. One of the largest centres, of the Nasca phase, is a group of at least six, each accompanied by courts, but they are natural hills, terraced and faced with conical adobes. Even so, they do not approach the entirely artificial pyramids of the north in size.

An ability to delineate outline figures on a vast scale is demonstrated by the markings seen from the air on the desolate pampas round the Nasca Valley *(Ill. 172)*. There is an immense number of long, straight lines, also rectangles, triangles, spirals, zig-zags and occasional birds and fish, formed by removing the dark brown pebbles which cover the yellow, sandy surface. The animal forms recall some painted on Nasca pots, and a radiocarbon date of about A D 500, measured on a post associated with them, connects them with the Nasca phase. Their use is uncertain—astronomical

178

172 Markings on the barren plateau above the Nasca Valley. Linear patterns have been formed by removing surface pebbles to expose the yellow sandy soil. Nasca Culture

observations have been suggested—but it must surely have been a ceremonial one.

The end of Classic times is heralded by changes in the Nasca pottery style, which began about the eighth century, mainly by degeneration but partly by the appearance of new influences. Drawing becomes slovenly, background colours dull, there is a tendency to geometrical decoration, and modelled forms of birds, animals and human beings, previously very rare, become more frequent.

THE SOUTH HIGHLANDS

Important remains of the later Formative and Classic periods have been found in three places, Tiahuanaco, Pucára and Chiripa, and isolated examples of stone carving are scattered throughout the region.

At Chiripa, on the Bolivian side of Lake Titicaca, a group of double-walled rectangular adobe houses was found ranged round a court, and they were accompanied by thick-walled pottery painted with steps and similar geometrical designs in yellow on a red slip, which suggests the beginning of painted decoration like the white-on-red of the coast. Most examples are flat-based bowls with vertical sides. The site is dated to the first six centuries B C.

Much more important are the other two sites. The famous site of Tiahuanaco, also on the Bolivian side of the lake, had a long life, from well back in the Late Formative Period until after the Classic. The extent of its influence on the whole region in early Post-Classic times is one of the most notable features of American archaeology. Little has been published about the earliest stages, but it is known that there was incised and painted pottery, possibly related to Paracas. The oldest stone structures seem to date from the last centuries B C and to be contemporary with the pottery generally called Early Tiahuanaco. This includes a polychrome ware decorated in shiny black, white, red, orange and brown, directly on the micaceous brown clay or on a slip of the same colour, with interlocking geometrical designs such as triangles, or strange highly stylized animal forms. The vessels are flat-bottomed, and typical shapes are an open bowl with slightly diverging sides and wavy rim, bearing a modelled feline head and tail *(Ill. 173)*, the 'spittoon', and a tall-necked bottle. The feline heads already show the eye divided vertically into black and white halves, which is highly characteristic of the art style of the area. Similar shapes, apart from the spittoon, continued into the Classic Period. There are concave-sided bowls with feline heads and tails, but the head is more realistic though it issues from a square flange. There are similar bowls with plain rims which may have a pair of ring handles on the sides, but the most typical of all is a new form, a tall, graceful, concave-sided beaker, the *kero (Ill. 174)*, which may have a raised cordon round the middle. Vessels generally have a red slip, which gives them rather a sombre appear-

173 Bowl with feline head and tail and wavy rim, painted in red, black, white, orange and brown on pale brown ware. Note the divided eyes. Early Tiahuanaco, Formative Period. South Highlands

174 Beaker *(kero)* with upper band of stylized heads, lower of stylized felines, all in profile. Note vertically divided eyes. Polychrome paint on red slip. Classic Tiahuanaco

ance, over which they are painted in yellow, grey or brown, black and white, or some of these colours. The ware is fine and well polished, but the design colours, originally bright, may weather rather faint. The most usual designs are felines and condors in profile with divided eyes, and geometrical figures such as steps, triangles and the combined angular scroll and step called the step fret. The felines show a stylized nostril looking like a ring balanced on the snout. After the Classic Period the pottery passed into a decadent stage which lasted for an unknown time. Designs were carelessly painted, geometrical ones became more frequent, and animal forms broke down so that eyes or heads appeared repeatedly instead of whole figures. Shapes also changed, and in particular the *kero* became less graceful, some examples having a very small base, a feature which may have spread from the Cochabamba district where it appeared in Classic times.

Tiahuanaco is primarily known for its masonry and stone carving. Already in the Late Formative there was a rectangular platform with a retaining wall of massive dressed uprights alternating with a filling of smaller rectangular blocks, but most of the other surviving structures, which are greatly damaged by the looting of stone, are probably of Classic date. Their relationships are somewhat haphazard, and the site does not compare in its planning with the great Mesoamerican ones. There is a large rectangular stepped pyramid with smaller ones projecting from it on opposite sides, made by improving and facing a natural hill, and this was crowned with a reservoir as well as buildings. There is a semi-subterranean rectangular building with carved heads tenoned into the walls, and there are a number of remarkable large stone blocks, carved with great accuracy and skill, some of which have doorways, rectilinear niches, and such figures as stepped squares and rectangles, recessed or in relief. Some of these may have been assembled to form chambers with monolithic walls, and some to form larger buildings. Some stones were held together by accurately cut notches, and some by straight or T-shaped copper cramps recessed into the stones, and it has been suggested that tools of hardened copper must have been

175 Central figure from monolithic doorway, holding staves thought to represent a spear-thrower, and a quiver of darts. Probably an important god. Classic Period. Tiahuanaco, Bolivia

used to shape at least the notched ones, although most Andean masonry was worked with stone tools. Perhaps the most notable feature of the site is the great monolithic doorway, cut from a block of lava about 12 feet by 10 feet, bearing a central figure carved in low relief, flanked by three rows of attendants, with a border at the bottom bearing complex frets ending in condor heads and enclosing heads like those of the central figure *(Ill. 175)* This figure stands facing the front and holding a staff in each hand. The hands have only three fingers and the thumb. The staves, which may represent a spear-thrower and a quiver with two darts, have a condor head at the lower end, and one has a condor at the top to represent the hook of the spear-thrower, whereas the other bifurcates and both halves end in a condor head. The trapezoidal head is surrounded by radiating appendages,

176 Kneeling
statue of limest
Probably Late
mative. Pok
near Tiahuar
Bolivia

which appears on the pottery, and the remainder end simply in rings. The face has round staring eyes from which depend bands bearing circles, which suggest tears. Condor and feline heads are repeated on the body, and from the belt hangs a row of faces, perhaps trophy heads. The attendants, who face in towards the central figure, have heads like his, but in profile, or condor heads, and are dressed in winged cloaks bearing numerous condor head appendages. They also carry staves. The weeping eyes, the standing figure himself, the condor and the feline, represented so differently from the felines of Chavín, are features which recur constantly wherever the influence of Tiahuanaco is felt and must lie at the heart of its religion.

Massive statues have been found in and around Tiahuanaco, the largest being 24 feet in total height. They resemble pillars bearing relief designs rather than true sculpture in the round; clothing is shown in flat relief like the subsidiary figures on the great doorway, and the figures may carry beakers or unidentified objects. The flat relief carvings on statues and doorway may reasonably be supposed to have been derived from textile patterns, and although no highland Tiahuanaco textiles have been preserved, similar designs appear on coastal ones under Tiahuanaco influence. Classic Tiahuanaco pottery lacks some designs found on the stonework, such as the full-face standing figure, which appear on coastal pottery and textiles, and it is thought that textiles were the main vehicle for the transference of Tiahuanaco designs to the coast. Apart from the pillar-like statues there are slabs with relief designs and tenoned heads for insertion into walls at Tiahuanaco. Some of the slabs and a few statues show carving in rather a different style, sub-angular or heavily rounded rather than angular, which resembles Late Formative examples at Pucára, so it probably precedes the typical Tiahuanaco style. Kneeling statues by the churchyard at Tiahuanaco and at Pokotia are examples *(Ill. 176)*.

Tiahuanaco art, then, is stiff and formal with a limited repertory. Even living creatures are heavy and squat, and in the Classic Period all show a strong tendency to rectilinear forms. The sculptures and probably the buildings themselves were originally painted

177 Stone statue showing a man carrying a
human head. Late Formative. Pucára, South
Highlands, Peru

and some details appear to have been sheathed with gold plates,
but this may well have accentuated the impression of massive
severity which is given even by the scattered remnants of the
ceremonial site.

Pucára is some way north-west of Lake Titicaca, and dates
from the end of the Late Formative between about 250 B C and
A D 100. The chief sanctuary here consisted of a horseshoe-shaped
enclosure, bounded by at least two concentric walls composed
of short, straight lengths with red sandstone foundations. The
outer one enclosed small chambers containing one or two altar-
like slabs in its thickness. Within the enclosure was a slightly
sunken terrace surrounding a square sunken court bounded by

white sandstone slabs. The masonry is not so well fitted as that of Tiahuanaco, and chinks may be filled with adobe or pieces of stone. The buildings themselves have vanished, but are thought to have been of adobe with thatched roofs.

The sculptures consist of statues and flat standing slabs. The typical statues are squat, heavy men wearing a cap and a loin-cloth with side flaps, and they may also carry a human head *(Ill. 177)*. Their sub-angular contours have already been mentioned. Many of the slabs have a notch cut out of one side at the top, and are carved in low relief with geometrical figures made up of checkers, stepped crosses, sharp zig-zags, diamonds and chevrons, with curvilinear patterns whose flow is interrupted by zig-zags, or with stylized fresh-water fish or lizards.

The decorated pottery, which is known only from fragments, is made of a reddish-buff micaceous clay, and designs are painted in red and black on the natural colour, or in black and rather fugitive yellow over a red slip *(Ill. 178)*. A characteristic feature is that the outlines of the colours are incised. Designs include felines in profile with the head shown full face in relief, human, feline and condor heads in profile, and geometrical figures such as stepped lines. As at Tiahuanaco, eyes are divided vertically, but the natural buff of the ware may replace the white used there,

178 Potsherd representing feline head with vertically divided eyes. Design in low relief, incised and painted in black and red. Late Formative. Pucára, South Highlands, Peru

and nostrils may be shown as rings balanced on the snout. Known shapes are a flat-bottomed bowl with flaring sides and a bowl with a low ring base, and what appears to be part of a trumpet. By the time that Tiahuanaco had reached its full flowering, Pucára seems to have been abandoned.

Early Post-Classic : The Tiahuanaco Spread

The end of Classic times is thought to have been marked by general unrest, during which the Tiahuanaco ceremonial pottery style appeared among the native ones in the Mantaro basin, and notably at the extensive site of Huari, which lacks important buildings. It was transmitted thence to the coast, probably in the tenth century, where it is found at Nasca and Pachacámac. The best examples come from Pacheco in the Nasca Valley, where a great dump of broken ceremonial pottery was found. Among the forms reconstructed are large inverted bell-shaped urns with flattened bases, painted in polychrome with full-face standing figures with divided eyes, closely resembling the central figure on the Tiahua-naco doorway. There are also large boldly-painted human effigy jars, and others in the form of a llama. A common feature here and on the central coast was a band of painted chevrons, forming a border or decorating the bridge of a double-spouted jar.

To begin with, the style was everywhere strongly Tiahuanacoid in character and comparatively uniform, with a similar range of colours to the highland style but brighter in tone. Some features of highland sculpture, especially the full-face standing figure, his face alone, and the attendant figures, appear on coastal pottery but not on that of Tiahuanaco itself. The same designs are found on coastal tapestries, but stone sculpture is totally lacking there. There are differences in detail between the two areas, for instance feline heads may replace condor ones, and the 'tear' bands on the face may be shown ending in trophy heads, but there is no doubt as to the identity of the figures. Pottery shapes also differ, but two are common to coast and highlands, the *kero* and a cup of more squat proportions, though the coastal *kero* was straight-sided and less graceful.

179 Poncho shirt, with vertical bands of tapestry bearing abstract designs. The vertically divided eyes show the derivation from Tiahuanaco. Coast Tiahuanaco, Early Post-Classic Period

180 Process of stylization from one of the falcon-headed, staff-bearing attendant figures on the monolithic gateway, Tiahuanaco *(left)*, to textile designs. This process can be more easily understood if the figure

After a comparatively short time, perhaps half a century, each of the three main centres, Huari, Pachacámac and Nasca, developed its own variety of Tiahuanaco-influenced pottery which spread through its own area. (The Pachacámac variety, which spread south to Ica, favoured the depiction of birds of prey.) The old artistic traditions were obliterated, and the Nasca and Interlocking styles vanished for ever. Tiahuanacoid influence spread far to the north, and the Mochica style also disappeared, though it reappeared later in a degenerate form, which suggests that it may have lingered on in remote northern regions as yet unexplored. After this the Tiahuanaco style gradually faded away, and this was shown on the pottery by a breakdown of Tiahuanaco designs and a reduction in the number of shapes and colours.

This, then, was the general sequence of events. The reasons for them are not certain, but the earliest contacts between highlands and coast, involving the transfer of religious symbols, can best be explained as a religious movement. The next stage, with its obliteration of the older art styles throughout the coast and the introduction of new building plans and the southern custom of burial in cloth-wrapped bundles to the Mochica area, strongly suggests military force emanating from Huari or the central coast. The north highlands were also affected, but by contact rather than conquest, except for a possible brief intrusion into the Callejón de Huaylas. Then came the gradual fading of Tiahuanaco influence,

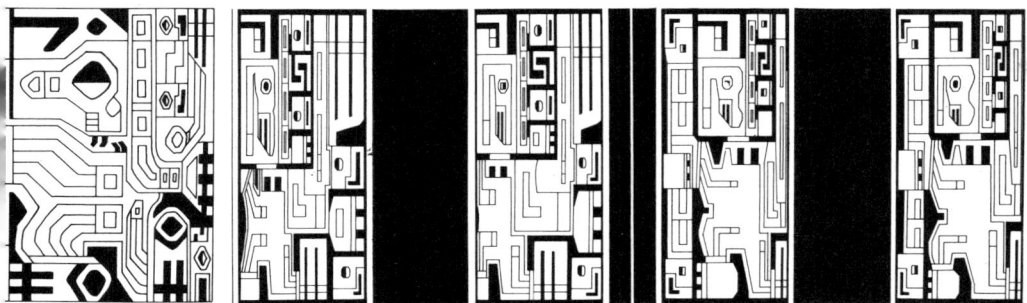

is regarded as a series of vertical zones which can be extended, contracted, or even transposed at will. The most contracted form can be seen on the right. Coast Tiahuanaco Culture

perhaps by the absorption of the invaders, over a period of two to three centuries, followed by the emergence of three new coastal states. A few significant features of coastal Tiahuanaco art can now be discussed.

Textile production flourished. Tapestries bearing designs closely similar to those of the highland stonework have already been mentioned, but there are others in which the designs appear to be abstract, although most of them retain obvious Tiahuanaco motifs, such as divided eyes, executed in various colours. They belong to poncho-like shirts, on which the designs appear on a varying number of broad vertical bands symmetrically disposed about the central line, and it has been ingeniously suggested that they may have been a kind of uniform for officials, the grade denoted by the number and width of the ornamental bands *(Ill. 179)*. The designs are executed mostly in yellows, oranges and light browns, with a limited use of blue, green, red and pink, and, to take an example, steps in stylization have been traced from a close copy of one of the attendant figures on the Tiahuanaco doorway to an unrecognizable abstraction *(Ill. 180)*. If the figure is thought of as a series of vertical zones, some may be widened, some compressed, and some even transposed. In certain instances the process has gone so far that not even eyes remain, and the design's units may consist of some such pattern as a square with a pair of step frets balancing about a diagonal. Another interesting technique

was knotted pile cloth, used to make square caps *(Ill. 181)*, some of which were decorated with Tiahuanacoid figures with divided eyes. Similar caps were made in feather-work. Tie-dyeing *(plangi)* was used to produce rows of irregular hollow circles of the colour of the undyed cloth against a dyed background, and a patchwork of pieces of different colours is sometimes found.

Apart from the *keros* and cups already mentioned, common forms of painted pottery are double spout and bridge jars with rather long tapering spouts, which diverge much more sharply than Nasca ones *(Ill. 182)*, and jars with a modelled face on the neck. Painted designs, at first of clear Tiahuanaco character, break down in time and the end product is geometrical decoration in black, white and red *(Ill. 183)*, which in some cases can be seen to be the final degeneration of faces or figures. Monochrome black, grey or red wares decorated in relief by casting in pottery moulds (pressed relief) are common. The designs may take such forms as step frets or running scrolls, or sunken pictorial panels with such features as cats or men holding staves in low relief against a stippled background. Shapes are very varied and include canteen-shaped

182 Double spout and bridge vessel decorated with a falcon-headed, staff-bearing figure with wings. Coast Tiahuanaco Culture

183 Bowl with animal head, rudimentary limbs and tail in relief, and painted with geometrical designs in black, white and red. End of Coast Tiahuanaco Period. Probably Central Coast

bottles, double vessels and double spout and bridge jars. Some of these designs and shapes carry over into the later Chimú black ware. Characteristic of a late stage, especially in the north, is a red to buff coloured face-collar jar, painted in very washy black, white and orange, which may have pressed relief designs on the body *(Ill. 184)*.

A good many small objects in wood, shell, stone, bone or metal have been found in Coast Tiahuanaco graves or show characteristics of the period, but some would be hard to distinguish from those of the next stage. Many of them have multi-coloured inlays, showing great skill in the handling of the materials, and it is this, rather than any great artistic merit, which gives them their chief interest. There is little to say about coastal architecture, except that the southern invasion of the Virú Valley on the north coast was accompanied by the introduction of large rectangular adobe-walled compounds without interior divisions, as well as smaller ones enclosing groups of dwellings, which may foreshadow the urbanization of the following period.

The situation in the north highlands was different. Pottery belonging to a middle Coast Tiahuanaco stage is found with local wares in stone-lined graves in the Callejón de Huaylas, in probable association with some stone buildings, which are the only reason for drawing attention to the area. The most elaborate of these, now sadly decayed, is at Wilkawain. It has three storeys, each with seven rooms with ventilation shafts; it is of split but undressed stone, in alternating thick and thin courses, with the interstices filled with small stones. It is crowned with a projecting course of slabs, with a recessed one beneath it, below which was a row of tenoned cat heads, none of which are now in place. This is local masonry, with a remote resemblance to Chavín but none to Tiahuanaco, and the presence of the Coast Tiahuanaco pottery cannot mean more than a brief intrusion at the most.

Further north, in the highlands east of the Chicama Valley, is a great fortified hill-top group called Marca Huamachuco, which owes nothing to Tiahuanaco. It is skilfully built of irregular coursed rubble, with long-and-short quoins like those of late

184 Face-collar jar. On neck, head of man wearing hat and ear-spools; on body, felines in pressed relief. Painted in washy black, white and orange on buff ground. Late North Coast Tiahuanaco style

Saxon work in England, and some buildings had two or three storeys. The usual building unit was a long narrow gallery, with the upper floors normally supported on corbels, and some of these were arranged round courts and some placed irregularly. The outer wall of the main group is double, and itself forms a gallery round the perimeter. There was some ornamental stonework, including stylized feline heads with zig-zag crests, which might be a reminiscence of Recuay, tenoned for insertion into walls, and some small slabs with step frets in low relief. The main building period here is associated with painted pottery of Cursive style, related to that of Cajamarca in the same region.

Cajamarca itself was slow to be affected by Tiahuanaco. Pottery of north coast Tiahuanaco styles has been found there, but the local cursive manner of painting on white or cream paste continued and only the designs gradually changed under Tiahuanaco influence until there came to be a majority of carelessly drawn feline heads and circles, possibly representing eyes or jaguar markings. The original Cursive tradition remained strong enough to influence a north coast pottery style at the beginning of the next period.

The Later Post-Classic

Tiahuanaco influence on the art of the south coast died out by about A D 1100, though it may have lasted longer in the north, but by the thirteenth or the beginning of the fourteenth century new states were established on the coast, and each had its own pottery style, although there were few obvious differences in metalwork and textiles.

In the north was the kingdom of Chimú or Chimor, with its capital at Chan Chan near Trujillo; it is thought that there was an older independent state to the north of it, with its centre in the Lambayeque Valley, but this was absorbed by the Chimú in the fifteenth century. Insofar as they are known, its architecture and pottery were similar to those of Chimú—in fact this may be the one area where the north coast modelling tradition survived the Tiahuanaco spread. Chan Chan contained ten great compounds surrounded by walls, in some cases double, with few openings, of rectangular adobe bricks or cast adobe *(tapia)* up to 50 feet high, separated by irrigated areas, cemeteries and minor buildings. Each compound was carefully planned, and might include small pyramids, rows of houses and store-rooms, gardens sunk to the water-table, and stone-lined reservoirs. Some also contained imposing buildings with walls covered with designs in moulded clay plaster *(Ill. 185)* believed to be the dwellings of the nobility, who had concentrated their retainers in the com-

185 Relief on a wall in the fortress of Chan Chan. Bands of birds, fish, and fantastic animals, and of scrolls and step-ornament. Moulded clay plaster. Chimú Culture. Later Post-Classic Period

pounds in order to control them. The designs vary a good deal; they include bands of step frets and scrolls, trellises, and comparatively realistic birds, fish and animals, as well as highly stylized bird designs like some of the Chimú textile patterns. Other important towns were similarly laid out. Large pyramids do not appear to have been built in this period, and those associated with some towns, *e.g.* Pacatnamú in the Jequetepeque Valley, are probably older. The question is complicated by the weathered state of the ruins, but the absence of imposing religious structures in important towns is in any case an indication of increased secularization. At the southern limit of Chimú, in the Fortaleza Valley, is a great terraced structure of rectangular adobes crowning a hill, which is believed to have been a frontier fortress.

186 Hammered silver double spout and bridge ceremonial vessel with ornamental band on body, openwork crest on bridge and freestanding elements in the form of two monkeys and four heads. Chimú. Lambayeque Valley

187 Drinking vessel *(paccha)* in the form of a man fishing from a reed raft. Black ware. Chimú

188 Black ware canteen, with pressed relief showing a jaguar on body, and two small handles. Chimú

189 Stirrup-spouted vessel with monkey on spout and a man holding a child, model-led in the round, on a cubical base. Black ware. Against a background of a contemporary buff textile with brocaded fish and pelican designs. Chimú

Chimú is known for its polished black modelled pottery, which has been likened to tarnished silver *(Ill. 189)*, and some well known pottery shapes are occasionally found in silver *(Ill. 186)* or gold, to which they seem well suited. The stirrup-spouted jar is a common form, but the spout differs from Mochica and older forms in that the loop tends to have a rectangular section, its sides may have a row of birds in pressed relief, and a small animal, usually a monkey, is perched on the junction between this and the upright. The body of the pot may be of a simple form, commonly spheroidal, in some cases with panels in pressed relief, *(Ill. 188)*, or it may be modelled to represent a wide variety of forms such as human and animal figures, heads, limbs, vegetables, houses or rafts *(Ill. 187)*. There are many other shapes, such as canteens, double spout and bridge jars or similar ones with one spout replaced by a head or figure, and double jars which may whistle, but in spite of the variety of subjects there is much standardization and a depressing lifelessness about the modelling, which is much inferior to most Mochica work. Pottery, metalwork, textiles and other products are thought to have been made under conditions something like mass production, and this is supported by the finding near Chan Chan of a workshop containing vast numbers of shell fragments at all stages in the production of inlay for wooden carvings *(Ill. 192)*. Although black pottery predominates, red ware in similar forms is also found, and Kubler has suggested that the modelled forms as well as the pressed relief were selected under the influence of metal-working, comparing the red ware to copper as he did the black to tarnished silver. There are smaller quantities of some painted wares, in dull red on white, and black or black and red on a dull reddish buff. The first two differ only in colour from the black ware, and the third, nearly all spout and figure jars, has black cursive decoration divided into zones by thin red bands. The painting points to influence from Cajamarca and some of the modelling may even point, at a long remove, to Recuay.

A good deal of the surviving metalwork is thought to be Chimú, but some of it cannot be located either in place or time so this brief

190 Repoussé gold beaker decorated with a standing male figure with plumed head-dress and ear-spools, holding staffs. The head-dress and the ear-spools are inlaid with turquoise. Chimú. Lambayeque Valley

summary must cover a wider range. There are graceful *Kero*-shaped beakers with repoussé designs *(Ill. 190)*, narrow nearly cylindrical ones of surpassing ugliness with a beaky face on one side, diadems, attractive little cast ear-scoops with a bird or animal on the top, knives, mace-heads, open-work crescentic-shaped nose-ornaments, model litters and a host of other things in gold, silver, copper and their alloys *(Ill. 193)*. Bronze probably dates from the Inca period. Silver objects may be inlaid with gold, copper

Gold funerary mask with stone eyes and traces of red and green pa
Chimú. Lambayeque Valley

ones with silver and bronze ones with copper and silver. There
are wooden figurines inlaid with gold and shell, and wooden
spear-throwers sheathed in gold. Thin plaques and sequins were
made for sewing to garments, and ear ornaments, pectorals and
even mummy masks had danglers attached to catch the light.
The effect in some cases, particularly when the metal is very thin,
verges on the tawdry. Some of the most elaborate and flamboyant
objects come from the far north *(Ill. 191)*, and among them are
large gold ceremonial knives with semicircular blades from the
Lambayeque area. A good example has a plain handle with
danglers at the top, surmounted by the hollow figure of a deer
(Ill. 194). A type of which several are known has a handle consisting of a hollow dumpy figure with a large semicircular head-
dress, which must represent a god or ruler. His eyes, ears and

192 Ear-spool with a reversible design of two birds with a common body. Wood, with crenellated and polished edge, inlaid with coloured shell. Chimú

193 Thin silver, repoussé ear-spools showing a central head with head-dress, surrounded by ten similar heads. Chimú

194 Ceremonia
knife. The blad
has a semicircula
tip and is su
mounted by th
hollow figure of
deer, and dangler
Blade of base met
with gold overla
ornamentation
gold. Chimú. Lan
bayeque Valley

195 Painted plain weave cotton textile. Designs are in brown on a buff ground, originally white. Chimú. Painted designs of this time show far less sureness of touch than woven ones (cf. *Ills. 196, 197*)

clothing may be inlaid with turquoise and his face painted red with cinnabar.

Some of the pleasantest products of the period are textiles, but even here there is a tendency to standardization *(Ills. 195-8)*. A great variety of techniques was known, but gauzes, brocades and double cloth were particularly common, and tapestry, formerly so popular, was confined to small areas such as corners and narrow borders. The products of different parts of the coast can be distinguished by specialists, but there is an overall similarity and what is said here about Chimú can be applied to other areas. Birds, especially pelicans, fish and animals, were stylized in an almost uniform and very competent fashion, and arranged in horizontal or diagonal rows, or in the contrasting colour on squares or diamonds of two alternating colours, a type of design to which double cloth is particularly suited. Step frets were commonly used for borders. Feather-work was very popular; feathers of different colours were sewn to plain weave cloth to produce a sort of mosaic, making designs such as scrolls, birds, animals and fish. It was used on poncho shirts, and to make diadems, and similar mosaic designs are also found on the ends of wooden ear-plugs.

196 Double cloth with pelican designs in brown and white *(below)*. The border of tapestry is worked on gauze with pelicans within scrolled lozenges. Chimú

197 Doll representing fisherman and net. Slit tapestry face, and warp-striped plain weave shirt, in pink, white, black, buff, yellow, green and pale lavender. Chancay Valley, Central Coast

198 How to draw a cat. Warp-striped textile with brocaded cats in blue, yellow and brown on dirty white. Chimú

On the central coast was a state called Cuismancu, much smaller than Chimú, which occupied the Chancay, Ancón, Rimac and Lurín Valleys. It is chiefly distinguished by its pottery style, which takes its name from Chancay *(Ill. 199)*. It is a dull red or cream ware with a crumbly white slip over which simple designs such as stripes, wavy lines, cross-hatching, chevrons, dot-sprinkled

199 Large ovoid jar with black-on-white decoration. Chancay style, Later Post-Classic. Central Coast

triangles or small animals are painted in black. It grew out of a black-white-red style *(Ill. 183)*, or degenerated from it, and some examples retain red bands. Typical shapes are large ovoid jars with a flaring or cup-like collar and a pair of loop handles, and effigy jars of much the same shape, with rudimentary limbs and a curious flat face with a pointed chin on the collar. There are also bowls of various shapes and double jars with a spout, bridge and figure on the top. Although this is ceramically and artistically a degenerate style, it has become fashionable among collectors.

The architecture of Cuismancu is less known than that of Chimú, but it seems to have been similar, since Cajamarquilla and Armatambo, both in the Rimac Valley, were large cities with walled compounds. Some of the walls have relief decoration, and some are crowned with battlements.

On the south coast another state called Chincha covered the valleys of Ica, Nasca, Pisco and Chincha, with its capital in the Ica Valley. About A D 1100 a distinctive pottery style arose out of the disintegrated late Tiahuanaco variety sometimes called Epigonal, and it continued to develop up to the Inca conquest about 1475, and after it into early Colonial times. It covered the whole area but there were some minor variants in Chincha. The painted decoration, in black, white and red, was based on the repetition of small geometrical units, such as steps, crosses, squares, lozenges and zig-zags, or extremely stylized birds or fish which gave much the same effect. The patterns are clearly inspired by textiles. A common form is a bowl with a gently rounded base forming the maximum diameter, above which it slopes inwards to a somewhat constricted mouth encircled by a thickened and chamfered lip, which is highly characteristic *(Ill. 200)*.

200 Three bowls, painted with textile-inspired patterns in black, white and red. Note the thickened, chamfered lips of the outer bowls. Ica style, Later Post-Classic. South Coast

There is another form with much lower walls and no thickening of the lip, which gives a metallic impression. There are also numerous ovate jars with low necks and flaring lips, besides some with taller necks and a loop handle, and barrel-shaped canteens. The style shows much greater competence in design, material and colour than that of Chancay, and compares favourably with that of Chimú in being a new and vigorous style rather than a poor reflection of an older one.

Of the Post-Classic architectural remains in the southern valleys few are in good enough condition to show specific features and it is difficult to place them in the time sequence, apart from some of Inca style. The Tambo (guest-house) de Mora in the Chincha Valley, which may be of this age, had a large habitation area surrounding a ceremonial centre consisting of a court from which stairs led up to terraces, the whole flanked by two large pyramids. Tambo Colorado in Pisco is of uncertain date, though its good preservation shows that it must be late, and the trapezoidal doorways suggest that it may be Inca. There are long ranges of low adobe buildings, built with stone foundations on terraces on gently rising ground. They are plastered and painted red, yellow and white, and have doubly recessed niches of contrasting colours and openwork balustrades formed by setting adobes diagonally to form triangular openings. The site is probably the administrative centre of a small city.

Some buildings in the central and south highlands are worthy of mention. At many places in the Province of Canta, east of Lima, there are single-storey cylindrical towers of random masonry. They are apparently pre-Inca but are so well preserved that they are unlikely to be much older. The walls thicken upwards and are corbelled out both inwards and outwards, so the exterior expands somewhat towards the top, and a square central column, which also expands upwards, helps to support the slab roof. The chamber is generally empty, but mummy bundles may be buried beneath the floor. In the west of the same province, at Chipprak and other sites, there are rectangular towers of similar masonry which have one or more large trapezoidal niches extending the whole height of the façade, within which are small doorways of similar form. A small structure of similar form may be annexed to the main one. These buildings have subterranean chambers, some of them containing mummies, and the main chambers may have niches in the walls, which thicken upwards like those of the type previously described. These niches may contain crude pottery, and there may also be a fireplace with a chimney built in the thickness of the wall.

In the Titicaca Basin are the best-known *chullpas* or burial towers, of which the finest are at Sillustani. They may be round or square, faced with fine, dressed masonry or built entirely of random masonry. Most have the burial chamber inside them, but some of the rougher ones are solid and have the chamber underneath. They are believed to have been built by the Aymara people both before and after the Inca conquered them, and are associated with various crude pottery types which are thought to have developed out of the final stages of the Decadent Tiahuanaco style. The best *chullpas*, which show some resemblance to Inca masonry, have a plain projecting cornice and a corbelled vault.

THE INCAS

Although the Incas are believed to have settled at Cuzco at least as early as A D 1200, there was nothing notable about their art until they began to build up their empire in the middle of the fifteenth century.

All the known examples of the famous Inca masonry date from the Imperial period, and the idea of a rectangular urban lay-out, which was attempted at Cuzco itself, may well have been learnt from the Chimú after they were conquered between 1460 and 1470. Differences in the type of masonry are an indication of differences in function and possibly in origin, but not in age. The 'megalithic' type, made of large, perfectly fitted, polygonal blocks, is used for the retaining walls of terraces and for large enclosures, and there is a variety called cellular, of small polygonal blocks, which may also be used for buildings. It has been suggested that these were derived from rough stone walling, with the stones set in mud. The coursed ashlar type, built of rectangular blocks which generally have a somewhat convex surface with sunken joints, is used for buildings, and may have been derived from the turf construction which is still used for poor houses and field walls. Smooth ashlar, which was used for a few important buildings, was a refinement of this type. There are various intermediate varieties, and rectangular masonry can sometimes be seen surrounding a doorway in a cellular wall. Even the hardest stones, such as granite and syenite, are thought to have been pecked into shape with stone mauls.

The best example of 'megalithic' masonry is the great triple zig-zag rampart of the fortress of Saccsaihuamán, which crowns the hill overlooking Cuzco (Ill. 202). It is made of hard limestone and some of the stones in the lowest rampart are over 8 metres high. The finest ashlar is found in important temples, such as that of Viracocha, the sun and other gods, whose remains form part of the Dominican friary in Cuzco, where some of the stones were faced with gold plates. Even this had an essentially domestic plan, consisting of rectangular rooms set about a court within an enclosure. It has been described as a house of the gods made in the likeness of the houses of men. Buildings had little in the way of architectural ornament, although the thatched roofs are recorded to have been finely worked into patterns. They had trapezoidal niches, mostly in interior walls, and doorways of the same shape. They were usually long and low, some had two or rarely more storeys, but the upper one was in most cases a loft under the gabled roof. Most of the surviving remains derive their effect chiefly from their fine finish.

Machu Picchu, a town in the Urubamba Valley, contains a number of small ceremonial buildings of various forms, finely situated amid innumerable agricultural terraces on a saddle which falls steeply on either side to the river some 1,500 feet below. A striking feature of it is a low semicircular tower of the finest masonry which seems to grow out of the rock which it partly encloses (Ill. 201). Near by is a series of small stone basins

201 Machu Picchu. General view showing low semicircular tower of the finest masonry. Inca, after 1450

connected by drains, arranged one above the other up a steep hillside, a feature which recurs at other sites in the same area. Although they were not designed for effect, magnificent series of stone-faced agricultural terraces form some of the finest features

202 Lowest wall of zig-zag rampart of the fortress of Saccsaihuamán at Cuzco. Irregular 'megalithic' masonry. Inca, mid-fifteenth century

of this steep-sided valley in several places, and there are many similar instances elsewhere. In the head of a tributary of the Urubamba at Moray in the same neighbourhood are three large artificial circular depressions about 500 feet across. They are lined with concentric stone-faced terraces and make a most impressive sight. A circular group of five rooms facing onto a central court is recorded at Runcu Raccay in the same region, but the finest circular building of all was probably the tower reservoir, whose foundations alone survive, on top of the hill at Saccsaihuamán.

The same rather standardized type of building is found wherever the Inca conquests reached, from Ecuador to Chile and north-west Argentina. Stone was the material normally used for important buildings in the highlands, and on the coast adobe took its place, but the same trapezoidal niches and doorways are found there. Many of the coastal buildings were put up to dominate older sites like the sanctuary of Pachacámac, where a great terraced platform towers above the remains of the older shrine.

Although sculpture on a large scale does not survive, and indeed there may not have been any, many small stone objects were made and some are very pleasing. Miniature alpacas, with a hole in the back for offerings, are the commonest, and some of these are executed with a most competent economy of line *(Ill. 203)*. Low, flat-bottomed stone bowls are also found, and many of them have snakes in relief on the outer wall and a pair of loop handles, which may be replaced by animal-head lugs.

203 Hard black stone statuette of an alpaca with hole in its back. Similar models of pottery are still used for ceremonies to promote the fertility of the alpacas. Inca

Inca pottery was hard, well made and polished, and was produced in a few standard shapes. The painted ware has a number of minor variants, but all can be grouped under the name of Cuzco Polychrome. The usual colours are red, white, black and yellow, with orange sometimes added, especially in a variety found near Lake Titicaca. Designs are in most cases geometrical, for example diamonds, checkers, cross-hatching and rows of triangles, generally grouped in zones. A stylized plant design rather like a fish's backbone is sometimes present, and some attractive vessels are powdered with little animals, birds or insects *(Ill. 204)*. The most typical shape is a jar with a low conical base, domed body and tall, flaring neck called the aryballus *(Ill. 207)*. Originally a water or beer jar, it was carried on the back by a rope passing through two vertical strap handles low on the sides and over a nubbin high up between them, which was sometimes modelled to represent an animal head. It came to be made in smaller sizes down to about 6 inches high. Another painted form is a shallow platter with a bird's head or loop as a handle and a pair of minute projections on the opposite side of the rim. There were also jars of several shapes with wide strap handles.

204 Polychrome jar with lugs in the form of jaguars. A good Inca shape with somewhat unusual decoration which includes painted snakes. Inca, after 1450. Region of Cuzco

205 Provincial Inca aryballus, with stylized plant design in black on white, the base red. Chile

206 Provincial Inca aryballus in black ware with a pressed relief. Chimu-Inca style, after the Inca Conquest (*c.* 1470). North Coast

207 Cuzco polychrome aryballus decorated with geometrical patterns. Inca, after 1450

These shapes are found throughout the Empire, and modified forms of them were made in local wares, for instances a short-necked aryballus with pressed relief panels was made in Chimú black ware *(Ill. 206)*, and this and other Chimú-Inca forms tended to spread through the coast in the years before the Spaniards arrived. Another variant of the aryballus, with the conical base truncated, was made in polychrome ware in Chile *(Ill. 205)*. It is often possible to detect Inca influence in the shapes of necks and strap handles on other provincial vessels, like a fascinating hybrid from the Ica region in which both these features are present on a jar shaped like an Ica bowl with thickened rim passing up into a fluted dome *(Ill. 208)*. The course of events in the Ica Valley is particularly interesting, because the Inca conquest introduced an Inca pottery style, which took the place of the local one in important graves until the arrival of the Spaniards in 1534, when the local one regained its importance. This continued for 26 years before the effective occupation of the valley, during which interval the inhabitants felt that they had been liberated from the Inca yoke.

208 Hybrid Inca-Ica vessel painted black, white and orange. After the Inca conquest *(c. 1480)*. Ica Valley, South Coast

209 Polychrome vicuna wool tapestry poncho shirt. Inca. From an island in Late Titicaca

Inca textiles, like those of older periods, were made by many processes. There was a revival of the use of tapestry for the best work, which was of fine quality but still had a tendency to standardization. Typical Inca poncho shirts have a V-shaped area round the neck, which is treated differently from the rest *(Ill. 209)*; the main part may consist of a checker pattern, with the squares plain or adorned with geometrical figures, or it may have a repeating design like rows of feathers, and the V-shaped area may be bordered with small squares and powdered with small devices or left plain. Similar ponchos, distinguished only by the introduction of European foliage designs, were made after the Spanish Conquest.

210 Silver llama with gold appliqué. The red inlay of the saddle blanket has been restored. Inca

The most characteristic Inca metal objects which survive are small figures of silver, gold or combinations of them, representing llamas, alpacas or little naked men and women. These may be solid or hollow, and the human figures are more curious than beautiful though the animals may be very expressively rendered. (*Ill. 210*). Some bronze knives inlaid with silver and copper and adorned with cast heads or figures have also been found on Inca sites. Apart from these things, it is difficult to point to much that is specifically Inca; doubtless this is partly due to the destruction which has occurred since the Conquest, but it may partly be ascribed to an original paucity of indigenous Inca work, because it is known that the Incas brought Chimú artisans to Cuzco after subduing their country. In this, as in other matters, the Incas learnt much from the conquered peoples of the coast.

CHAPTER FIVE

A Glimpse of the South:
North-west Argentina and North Chile

These areas were finally incorporated in the Inca Empire, but
previously they were what has been justly described as a melting-
pot, in which influences from various quarters were fused to
produce some strongly individual results. Art is chiefly expressed
in pottery, metal and wood. There were forts and villages, largely
of dry stone walling, which scarcely deserve the title of architecture. Stone sculpture is reported, but too little is accessibly
published to allow any comment beyond a note that cylindrical
drinking vessels, with feline and human figures competently
carved in relief, are present in the Aguada Culture of what used
to be called the Diaguite region in the Argentine provinces of
Catamarca and La Rioja.

There are many indigenous pottery styles dating from about
200 B C onwards, but the important ones for our purposes are
after A D 700. The most notable, dating from A D 700 to 1000,
belongs to the same Aguada culture, formerly called Draconian
from the 'dragons' shown on the pottery. These are really deriv-
atives of the widespread Peruvian feline, mostly in a form which
suggests Recuay more than any other style, and there are two
main types, painted and incised. The first is oxidized and the
colours are black-purple-yellow, black-red-white, or simply black-
on-yellow. The second is reduced, grey or black, with the motifs
simply outlined, or outlined and hatched, or with the backgrounds
hatched giving a negative effect. Besides felines, there are birds,
frogs and human beings, some with axes and trophy heads. Painted
designs are generally shown with extreme liquidity, but the presence
of zig-zag lines in crestings and jaws gives an effect of angularity
to the incised ones even when the figures are composed largely
of curved lines. The pottery of the later Argentine cultures, after

211 Santa Maria urn, used for child burial, painted in black and red on cream slip. The design on the neck is a stylized face. Late Period, after AD 1000. Catamarca and neighbouring provinces, N. W. Argentina

AD 1000, is chiefly known for the funerary urns of Santa María and Belén in the same region. Santa María urns *(Ill. 211)* have an ovoid body with a pair of horizontal strap handles and a very tall flaring neck, and are decorated with striking geometrical designs in black on yellow or red on cream, mostly incorporating a highly stylized face recognizable from the eyes and the great arched brows meeting in a V, the only relief feature on the urn. Belén urns are similar but smaller, the neck is less exaggerated, and the painting is simpler and in black on red.

To the same late horizon belongs one of the most attractive pottery styles of Chile, which is found in the area immediately west of the home of the Argentine styles mentioned above, and is generally called Chilean Diaguite *(Ill. 212)*. The commonest form is a rather thick-walled bowl with rounded base and straight or slightly concave vertical sides, but there are also more complex forms such as jars with a head connected to a wide opening by a bridge. The painted decoration is in white, red and grey, and consists mainly of delicately-drawn step frets, checkers or hatched triangles, but there are some very simplified white rectangular faces sprinkled with grey dots with the mouth slightly raised. Relief is always at a minimum and confined to such features as mouths, noses or beaks. Finally there are some variants of Inca pottery of considerable charm which show their local origin in minor modifications of the standard shapes and in the style of painting. The aryballus *(Ill. 205)* mentioned in the chapter on Peru is a good example.

212 Chilean Diaguite bowl, painted in white, red and grey. Late Period, after AD 1000. North Chilean Coast, near Coquimbo

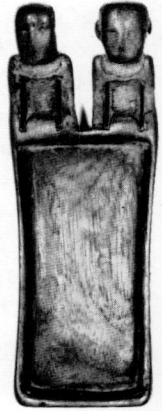

213 *(top)* Four carved wooden tablets and two tubes for taking snuff. Human and animal motifs, some of which show Tiahuanaco influence. Atacameño region, Rio Loa area, North Chilean Coast

214 *(below)* Cast copper plaque showing human figure between two felines. Aguada Culture, AD 700-1000, N.W. Argentina

Wood carvings are best preserved in the arid coastal Atacameño region of Chile, which lies north of the Diaguite area and adjoins the Peruvian border. Apart from undecorated utilitarian objects, the best examples are miniature trays and tubes for taking snuff, which have handles formed by cats, birds and human beings carved in the round *(Ill. 213)*, besides incised designs of Classic Tiahuanaco character and shell inlay. This is a southward extension of the Peruvian area, which not only marks the southern limit of direct Tiahuanaco influence but shows it in an unusually pure form.

North-west Argentina was a notable centre for metalwork, especially in copper, and was remarkable for the early appearance of bronze between A D 700 and 1000. The Aguada Culture has ceremonial copper axes with the head and the handle in one piece and the butt expanded into a crested feline head, a series of radiating spikes or some similar feature. Some fine and curious cast plaques, showing felines and human beings in relief, appear to belong to the same culture *(Ill. 214)*. Large copper discs with faces and other designs outlined by raised lines, in a manner much inferior to the plaques, probably belong to the later stage, after A D 1000.

CHAPTER SIX

Central America and the Northern Andes

The organization of this, the intermediate area between Mesoamerica and Peru, was simpler politically than theirs and it has
even been suggested that it remained on a Formative level.   Most
of it consisted of comparatively small units ruled by despotic chiefs,
and only in the case of the Chibcha in highland Colombia are these
units known to have formed a confederation.   In the later stages
the people normally lived in large villages with temples, but most
of these were of perishable materials.   More permanent structures
existed and examples will be given, but there was nothing to
compare in elaboration with the great ceremonial centres of the
nuclear areas.   On the other hand there was a notable mastery
of metalwork, which developed long before that of Mexico.

CENTRAL AMERICA
The area from the southern limit of intense Maya influence south
to the isthmus of Panama, now covered by the republics of
Nicaragua, Costa Rica and Panama, can be broadly treated as a unit,
within which the chief artistic developments took place after A D 500.
In many ways it belongs more to South than to Mesoamerica,
but influences from the north are never lacking.

   There is nothing very notable in the way of architecture, although
earth and stone mounds are sometimes ranged round courts,
and alignments of stone columns or statues are sometimes found.
Large stone carvings occur sporadically.   In south-west Nicaragua
there were tall statues of a man weighed down by a large animal
on his back, or else showing in a curious way his face looking
out from the animal's mouth, but we depend for our knowledge
of these on drawings made by early explorers.   Columns carved
rather rudely with human figures in low relief are reported from

215   Lava figure of a man eating a maize cob. Highland Costa Rica

Coclé Province, Panama. Smaller carvings are much better known. Finely carved stone club-heads, showing bird and crocodile heads among other designs, come from the Pacific coast of Costa Rica. From highland Costa Rica come standing or seated human figures, some showing a considerable degree of realism *(Ill. 215)*, but some, from the south highlands, are little more than a celt-shaped stone slab with a head and three slots separating the arms from the body and the legs from one another. Also from highland Costa Rica come thin rectangular slabs bordered at the sides with little figures in low relief and at the top with similar ones of monkeys or birds in the round; these were probably grave markers. Throughout Costa Rica and Panama there are beautifully carved *metates* or grinding slabs, standing on three or four slender legs or a complex support, some of which have a jaguar head and tail emerging from the ends *(Ill. 216)*. Of similar character are small circular objects like a miniature stool, on three legs or a central support, from highland Costa Rica and Chiriquí, Panama *(Ill. 217)*. Similar objects of wood and pottery have been found.

216   Stone grinding slab or *metate*.   Costa Rica

217 Miniature stone stool, Province of Chiriquí, Panama

On a miniature scale are large numbers of finely-worked objects of jade from Costa Rica and mainly of other stones such as agate from Panama. Highly typical of the jades are celt or knife-like objects with a human figure in low relief occupying the butt half of the blade *(Ill. 218)*, but there are also angular figurines, coiled snakes, magnificent cylindrical beads and many other forms. The angularity of the carving is a clear response to the way of working this very hard material by sawing and drilling. From Coclé, Panama, come many agate pendants representing skilfully stylized animals, especially monkeys with arched tails, and also plain bar-shaped pendants which rely for their effect on the colour and banding of the stone.

The most individual metalworking centres in the region were in Coclé and Veraguas, Panama; other centres in Chiriquí, Panama, and Costa Rica appear to derive from them, and they themselves have much in common with Colombia. Hemispherical gold helmets are known from both Colombia and Panama, and a notable example from Coclé is covered with intricate embossed designs showing the local crocodile god, which also appears on gold discs. The commonest technique is cire perdue casting, and a large

218 Grey-green jade celt with a human figure forming the butt. Nicoya, Costa Rica

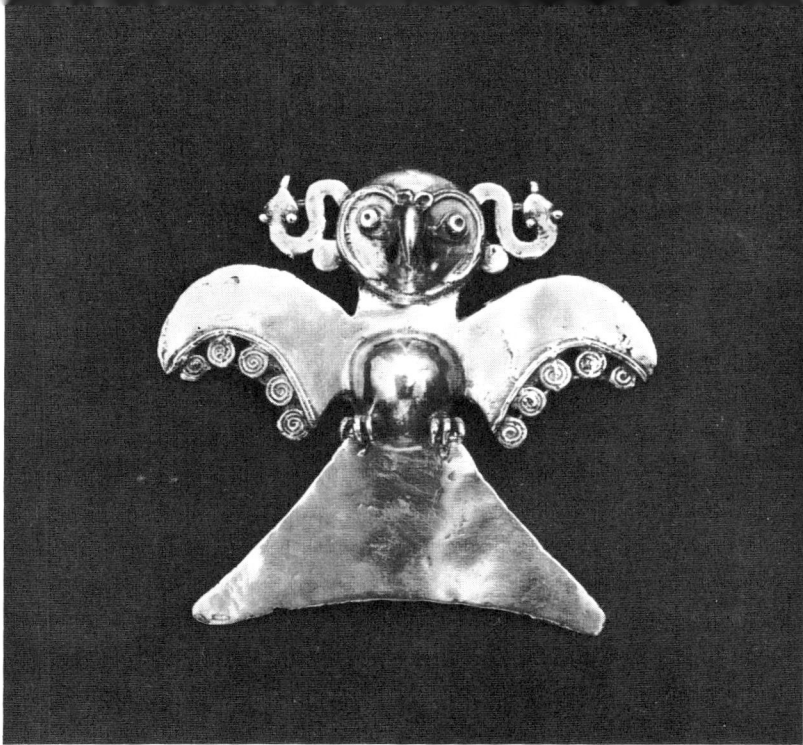

219 Gold pendant cast by cire perdue process. Bird with snake appendages. Veraguas Province, Panama

number of intricately decorated animals, monsters, bells, earspools and nose-clips were made in gold and the gold-copper alloys called *tumbaga*, which may be gilded by the mise en couleur process in which copper is leached from the surface with acid and the remaining gold burnished. Some of the most pleasing objects are of other materials combined with gold, such as earrods of agate, serpentine or opal with gold ends, and pendants made of a whale tooth with gold head and feet representing a bat or crocodile god. The most characteristic features of the Veraguas style are hollow castings with smooth, rounded contours spreading out at some points into sheets. Good examples are eagle pendants with great flat wings and tail *(Ill. 219)*, and frog pendants with large flat sub-rectangular hind feet. Men or gods stand on a rectangular flange, and have head-dresses of similar form. Most of these are gilded *tumbaga*, but some are gold.

220 Nicoya Polychrome tripod bowl with animal heads as feet. Pacific coast of Costa Rica

Only a few examples of the many pottery styles can be given. Among the most attractive are some types collectively called Nicoya Polychrome, from the Pacific coast of Costa Rica *(Ills. 220, 224, 225)*. Typical of this is an egg-shaped vessel with bulbous tripod feet *(Ill. 225)* or a ring base, decorated in black, red, orange, and rarely blue or purple, over a white to yellow slip. Some have a modelled head emerging from the side, generally a turkey, macaw or armadillo, other details of which may be shown in low relief or more usually in paint. Common painted designs show varieties of jaguar or plumed serpent, clearly derived from Mesoamerica, and some are shown in a pseudo-negative manner in the colour of the slip against a black ground. Other vehicles for such designs are figurines and bowls of various shapes, a common type being a shallow one with flaring sides and large animal heads forming

221 Globular jar with animal-head lugs, painted with two-headed alligator, in black, white and red. Alligator Ware, Chiriquí, Panama

222 Globular jar of Lost Colour Ware, with decoration in black negative painting over white and red. Chiriquí, Panama

tripod feet *(Ill. 220)*. Slightly different types of polychrome are found in the interior highlands *(Ill. 223)*, but they form a much smaller proportion of the pottery than on the Pacific coast. Among a profusion of one and two-coloured wares, whose distribution in time is only beginning to be worked out, are monochrome bowls standing on very tall tripod feet, generally in the form of an animal or fish, a type which extends into Chiriquí. Other notable Chiriquí wares, which are known to be of late pre-conquest date, are Lost Colour Ware and a polychrome called Alligator Ware. The first of these is decorated with simple negative designs such as dots and lines in rather fugitive black over a white or red slip or a combination of the two *(Ill. 222)*. It is used mainly for small objects such as jars and miniature double bowls. Alligator Ware is painted in black, white and red, and gets its name from the predominance of alligators and motifs connected with them *(Ill. 221)*.

One of the most remarkable pottery styles in a continent of remarkable styles comes from Coclé, Panama. It is found in the rich graves of that province and seems to have lasted, with minor variations, from at least the fourteenth century to the Conquest. There are plates, bowls and various types of jar decorated in white, red and black, to which may be added brown and purple, a rare colour on American pottery. The designs comprise scrolls, chevrons, birds, crocodiles, serpents, turtles and so on, frequently confined within zones or panels and drawn with a remarkable combination of sweeping boldness and delicacy of detail *(Ills. 226, 227)*.

223 Quadrangular tripod bowl with animal head and tail painted in black, white and red. Highland Polychrome. Costa Rica

224 Pottery figure of squatting woman wearing brassière, painted in black, white and red. Nicoya Polychrome. Pacific coast of Costa Rica

225 Ovoid tripod vase with applied animal head on side, the forelegs forming two of the vessel feet. Painted in black, white and red. Nicoya Polychrome, Pacific coast of Costa Rica

226 Pedestal dish, painted with crocodile heads and characteristic pointed hooks in red, black and purple on white. Coclé, Panama

227 Polychrome bottle, painted in black, red and purple on cream. Coclé, Panama

228 Coarse stone statue of a fanged human figure wearing a cap and loin-cloth, and carrying a staff and shield. San Agustín, Colombia

COLOMBIA

Colombia offers little in the way of architecture or stone sculpture. A group of sites round San Agustín, in the highland Department of Huila, forms an exception which has attracted much attention. They have small rectangular temples built of roughly-shaped stone slabs, enclosed in mounds rather like European megalithic tombs. Each contains a principal statue and several lesser ones, and the narrow open side forming the entrance may be flanked by caryatid figures. There are also subterranean galleries and tombs of similar construction. The statues are of various styles, which probably cover a considerable time-span. All are squat and some extremely so, some are carved in the round *(Ill. 228)*, some are slabs with details in low relief, and some are intermediate. Some have simple round eyes, in some they are a segment of a circle with the curve uppermost, and in some they are more realistically finished. Most have extremely wide nostrils, and large interlocking canine teeth like so many pseudo-feline faces in Peru and elsewhere.

237

They may hold a child, a snake, two staves, or other objects. Carvings are not necessarily moveable and rock outcrops, including a stream bed at Lavapatas, show figures, animals, snakes and many other forms. There is a single radiocarbon date of about 500 B C, but what point in the development of San Augustín it corresponds to is unknown. There has been much speculation about relations between this and other cultures from Nicaragua to Peru, and in some cases there is little but the trait of stone carving to connect them, but more precise dating may enable reliable conclusions to be drawn.

Colombia is a country of deep shaft graves, and the Tierradentro region in the Department of Cauca, north of San Agustín, contains some which are remarkable for their decoration *(Ill. 229)*. They are generally oval or round, some have columns left to support the roof, and some have niches. The shafts for access may have stairs cut in the rock. The chambers are covered with elaborate designs carved in relief or painted black, white, red and sometimes yellow; most are geometrical, but animal and human faces and figures also occur. Their age is not known, nor is their relation to statues and other carvings of San Agustín styles in the neighbourhood.

Colombia is renowned mainly for its metalwork, but little is known about the chronology of this or even of the most typical pottery styles. Great strides have been made recently in building up a cultural succession, but most of the metal comes from casual finds and grave-robbing, and much of the best pottery from unstratified, single-period sites. As in Central America, copper and *tumbaga* objects are as common as gold, and the same processes were used in working them. A number of regional styles have been distinguished, but some types, such as beads and ear-spools, were doubtless shared between more than one area, and the differences are blurred by trade. Perhaps the most distinguished style is the Quimbaya, of the Middle Cauca valley, known for the massive cire perdue gold castings in the British Museum and Madrid *(Ill. 231)*. There are graceful flasks, and figures of men and women with slit-like eyes, besides hemispherical helmets with embossed designs

229 View of interior of a shaft grave. Stone walls painted in several colours. Tierradentro region, Cauca, Colombia

in similar style. The finding of Quimbaya objects in Coclé, Panama, suggests a date within two or three centuries of the Conquest. Another attractive style is that of Calima, to the south-west of the Quimbaya and related to it. Typical of this are large kidney-shaped breast ornaments, with an embossed head in the middle having a large H-shaped nose ornament and ear-discs dangling from it. There are also masks, said to be for idols, diadems, elaborate crescent-shaped nose-ornaments with danglers, and cire perdue pins of *tumbaga* with little figures full of detail on the head. The general effect is one of rather barbaric profusion. On the strength of certain details it has been suggested that this style was contemporary with some San Agustín statues, but this needs substantiation. In the extreme north, towards Panama, the Darién style is distinguished by a most peculiar type of cire perdue casting of a semi-human figure with wide, plain, flat legs separated by a slit, contrasting with bat-like head and wings with intricate detail, in some cases so highly stylized as to be unrecognizable. The Province of Tolima, over the hills east of the Cauca Valley, has its own style. The characteristic feature is a gold or *tumbaga* pendant, flat except for the details of a face which appear to consist of applied strips but are actually cast by cire perdue. The flat body may have wings if it represents a bat, or angular limbs if a man or animal, and it generally ends below in a crescent with rounded ends. The bats have the body pierced with rows of slits and the edges cut into tatters. East of this area, around Bogotá, is the Chibcha or Muisca country, and this again has its own style, which has the least claim of all to artistic merit *(Ill. 230)*. Typical are flat or nearly flat plaques of gold or *tumbaga*, called *tunjos*, with a head and elongated triangular or quadrilateral body, with features, spidery limbs and insignia resembling applied wire, although cast by cire perdue. Groups of figures, pins, model spear-throwers and other objects were made in the same way. The impression they give is extremely crude, but some hollow human figures, conch shells and flat pendants with figures in relief are far superior in finish. Objects in Muisca style were being made at the time of the Conquest.

230 Gold figurine *(tunjo)*. A flat, human figure with wiry details wearing head-dress, carrying staff and shield, cast by cire perdue process. Chibcha, Colombia

231 Three objects of precious metal; a bell-shaped piece of uncertain use, decorated with a row of faces, a gourd-shaped flask, and a seated female figurine. Outer objects of *tumbaga* (gold-copper alloy), central one of gold. Quimbaya. Cauca Valley, Colombia

A few pottery styles deserve mention, mostly from the Quimbaya region. The first has negative painting in black over red (*Ill. 232*) or red and white, like that of the Lost Colour Ware of Panama, and it is doubtless related to styles showing the same technique in southern Colombia and Ecuador and, at a further remove, to Recuay in Peru. It is used not only on vessels but also on some examples of a curious, rather flat type of hollow figurine with a large, sometimes square head and spindly limbs, which generally squats or sits on a stool. Double vessels, spout and bridge and double spout and bridge jars are found in the same area; some are modelled in animal shapes, some are whistling jars and some are painted in red and white. These features point to the coast of Peru, but only generally because the details are very different, and in particular the form of loop-like bridge which unites the double spouts is found only here and in the neighbouring Calima district. Another unusual Quimbaya form of decoration is generally called champlevé; in it certain areas are differentiated by the deep excision of rows of small triangles or quadrilaterals *(Ill. 233)*.

Chibcha pottery does not reach a very high level, but it is worth mentioning because the use of applied strips of clay to show facial features and ornaments and spindly limbs in figure modelling, are recognizably connected with the type of decoration on the metal *tunjos*. This modelling is found on effigy vessels and hollow figurines, which are further decorated by incised lines and rows of circular reed impressions *(Ills. 234, 235)*. Much of the pottery is plain white, but some red painting on orange, buff or white is also found.

232 Bowl with black negative painting over red. Quimbaya, Colombia

233 *(above)* Red ware bowl with parts of the surface cut away after the manner of chip-carving, generally called champlevé. Quimbaya

234, 235 Two pottery heads, fragments of figurines, with applied, stamped and incised details. Chibcha, Colombia

ECUADOR

The population of Ecuador is and was concentrated chiefly in the highlands, a series of basins between the east and west chains of the Andes, and on the broad coastal plain to the west. The rise from the coast to the highlands is extremely sharp, and conditions in the two areas are so different that cultural expressions differ a great deal. Work done since 1954 has given a clear picture of developments on much of the coast, but the study of this region suffers in comparison with that of Peru because perishable objects are seldom preserved owing to wetter conditions.

Pottery appeared on the Ecuadorean coast at a surprisingly early date, between 3000 and 2500 B C, well before its beginning in Peru, and this is taken to mark the beginning of the Formative Period. No cultural remains of an earlier date are known in this zone. Three Formative sub-divisions, each thought to have been started by an invasion, have been recognized, and the third of these brought Mesoamerican elements, including some features found at Tlatilco. Like the Chavín style in Peru, these probably came by sea, because nothing like them has been found in the intermediate area and nothing is seen here of the feline cult which accompanies similar elements in Chavín. The next stage is called the Regional Developmental Period from the variety of intense developments which were reached in different sections, one of which, the Bahía Phase in Manabí Province, is judged to have attained a Classic level; this lasted from about 500 B C to A D 500. The final period, which lasted to the Conquest, has been called the Integration Period. It is marked by a simplification resulting in the establishment of three cultural types or phases covering the whole coast. More than three tribes were living there at the Conquest period so these types did not correspond to political units, although some of the tribes may have been closely related. Coastal Ecuador was exceptional in the Intermediate Area in having large towns in the more fertile parts.

Architectural remains are rare on the coast. The Bahía Phase has rectangular stone-faced platforms near the port of Manta, and there are earth mounds arranged in a U-shape round a court,

244

236 Standing male stone statue. Manteño Phase, Integration Period. La Pila, Manabí, coast of Ecuador

which may have formed a ceremonial centre, at La Tolita in Esmeraldas further north, an area under strong Mexican influence. In the latest period, the Milagro Phase in the inland Guayas Basin has numerous large earth mounds to support buildings in a flood-prone area and for burial purposes, but this is hardly architecture. Manabí Province was a centre of stone sculpture. There are stone slabs carved in low relief to show monsters, women accompanied by monkeys and men with birds, which are probably associated with the platforms of the Bahía Phase. In the latest period, the Manteño Phase has the famous U-shaped stone seats, carved in one piece with a crouching man or jaguar which supports them. Free-standing stone statues, most of which represent men wearing only a close-fitting head-dress with a flat or rounded top and either a breech clout or a narrow belt with two pendant strips down the thighs, belong to the same phase *(Ill. 236)*. These figures are much generalized; some have exaggeratedly square shoulders and the legs may be much too short or have squared outlines. Miniature versions are also found. These statues have been compared with those of San Agustín in Colombia, but they are very much more recent and the resemblances are too vague to inspire confidence. Statues which share some features with these, particularly the head-dresses, but with a peg base for setting in the

238 Two carinated bowls, pale brown to black and highly polished. The larger has pairs of faint pinkish iridescent paint running down the body, and the smaller has the outside of the rim painted red and dots of faint iridescent paint on the body. Formative Period. La Libertad, Guayas, coast of Ecuador

ground, are ascribed to a hill-top near Guayaquil, further south, but have all been moved. To the same Manteño Phase belong two remarkable wooden posts found in the area. The better of these, now in Guayaquil, has nine tiers of human figures, normally each of two men and two women with prominent genitals, alternating horizontally and vertically, but somewhat disturbed near the top by the insertion of two alligators. Some stone animal carvings have been found in the same neighbourhood. There is a crouching monkey of almost gorilla size at Chongón near Guayaquil, which is still an object of superstitious regard to the inhabitants, and a miniature bat, from La Libertad on the Pacific shore, shown with considerable skill by a minimum of shaping on a lump of dolerite (Ill. 237).

There is a great variety in Formative pottery on the coast, but taking it as a whole it depends for its interest on form and types of decoration such as application, incision and polishing rather than on colour, although there is a limited use of red and black painting and a peculiar inconspicuous iridescent paint is occasionally used for simple dots and stripes in a way which sometimes recalls negative painting. Some thin-walled, highly polished types were never rivalled in these respects, and in some cases the lustre seems to have been accentuated with iridescent paint

239 Three painted sherds, Guangala Phase, Regional Development Period, Province of Guayas, coast of Ecuador. One *(top left)* is from Guangala. Another *(top right)*, with stylized pelicans, is from La Libertad, as is the small sherd *(below)*

(Ill. 238). In the Regional Developmental Period, white-on-red and negative wares are found everywhere. The Bahía Phase, already mentioned, has polychrome wares and also painting done after firing which recalls the late Formative Paracas pottery of Peru, and its survival is remarkable in the wet climate of Manabí. The Guangala Phase of the Pacific coastal strip adjacent to Bahía on the south is distinguished by a thin, hard polychrome in black and red on yellow, showing pelicans and geometrical designs often derived from them. *(Ill. 239)*. This ware may be replaced locally by an equally fine two-colour chocolate on yellow, and there is a yellow type with bizarre faces and snakes in red outlined by engraved lines. Guangala also has a unique form of polypod bowl in unslipped red ware, with five or more pointed feet modelled to represent a human figure or face. Bahía is outstanding for the variety and interest of its figurines showing human beings and animals, some of them of Mexican derivation. It also has objects of very restricted distribution, such as head-rests, house models with swept-up ridge ends and certain figurines *(Ill. 241)*, which have been ascribed with some reason to the influence of a boatload of Asiatics who may have arrived about 200 B C. Guangala also has figurines;

248

they show far less variety than those of Bahía, though they are of related types, but they are generally superior in taste and finish. Among them is a hollow male figure wearing a domed cap and carrying a baby, which contains two whistles *(Ill. 242)*. The Integration Period is marked by a fashion for sombre coloured pottery, grey or brown, with incised, appliqué or pattern-burnished decoration *(Ill. 243)*. This is a curious parallel to the Chimú black ware of Peru and may be due to the development of mass production in both areas, but the expression is very different. The Milagro Phase in the Guayas Basin has a variety of fantastic bowls and jars with a profusion of appliqué figures of snakes, birds, lizards, frogs and human beings, probably for ritual purposes, which have been called 'witches' cauldrons'. Figurines continued to be made, especially in the Manteño Phase, but they are rather poor slab-like productions made in one-piece moulds *(Ill. 240)*. Face jars are common in the same phase *(Ill. 243)*.

240 *(left)* Slab-like grey pottery figurine of standing man with ear-spools and nose-ring. Manteño Phase, Integration Period. La Libertad, Guayas

241 *(right)* Hollow stone-coloured pottery figurine of standing woman with domed cap. Bahía Phase, Regional Development Period. Esmeraldas

242 Hollow whistle figurine of standing man wearing a swept-back domed cap and holding a child. Red-brown pottery largely smoked to dark grey. Guangala Phase, Regional Development Period

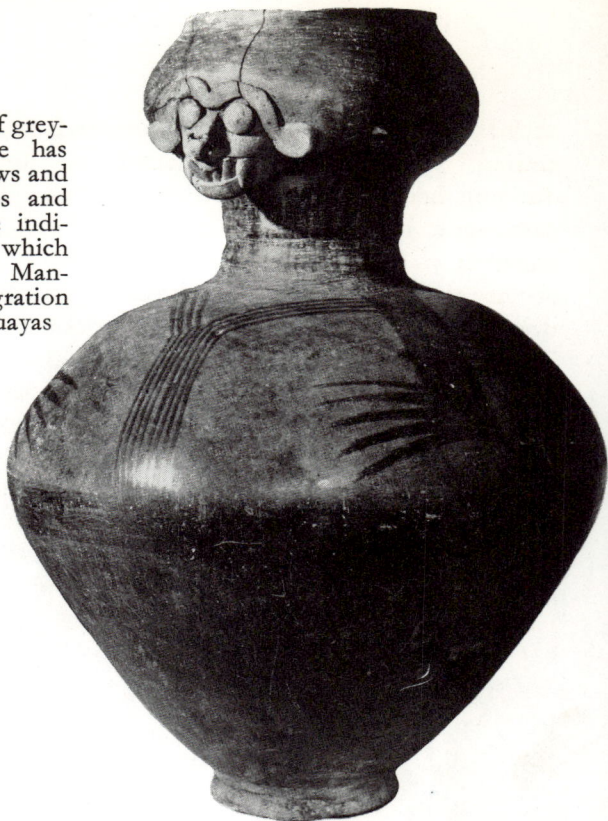

243 Face-collar urn, of grey-brown ware. Face has heavy applied eyebrows and fangs, and the limbs and perhaps clothing are indicated by burnishing, which darkens the surface. Manteño Phase, Integration Period. Salinas, Guayas

Metal was first worked in the Regional Development Period, but the bulk of the spectacular finds are of the Integration Period. Gold, silver and copper were worked, and Esmeraldas was remarkable for the working of platinum, which was combined with gold in some objects, for example it forms the eyes in some masks. Infusible at the available temperatures, grains of platinum were forged into a mass by repeated heating with a little gold dust, to produce an alloy of lower melting point, and hammering. The predominant decorative techniques were repoussé and the use of wire, and cire perdue was far less common than in Colombia and Central America. There are gold and silver bowls, helmets and collars all with repoussé decoration, and a multitude of smaller objects such as bracelets, beads, ear ornaments and nose ornaments, many of the latter composed of exceedingly elaborate arrangements of flat wire spirals. Turquoise discs were sometimes set in gold objects. Copper, sometimes gilded, was used for ornaments in the simpler burials.

A burial of the end of the Milagro Phase in the Guayas Basin was very rich in metal, and to this we owe evidence of the skill of the ancient Ecuadorians in making textiles, many of which were preserved by the copper salts. Few details are available, but the mention of warp and weft floats and fine *ikats* suggest that they were comparable in skill with the Peruvians.

It has not yet been possible to correlate the highlands with the coast except to some extent in the south, but they were on much the same artistic level. Apart from some Inca masonry in the south and older mounds in other parts, some for burial and some as sub-structures, there is nothing to show on the surface.

244 Pottery figurine head wearing high domed cap, ear-spools and nose-ring. Bahía Phase, Regional Development Period. Said to be from Esmeraldas, but probably from Manabí, coast of Ecuador

245 Bowl on low ring base, with black negative decoration showing outlines of two animals over cream and red. Tuncahuán style, El Angel, Province of Carchi, North Highlands of Ecuador

There are many pottery styles, among which that called Tuncahuán, with animal silhouettes and geometrical forms in black negative paint over red and cream *(Ill. 245)*, is related to Colombian negative styles. Rich finds of gold and copper, repoussé discs, nose ornaments, ceremonial gold axes, and so on, have been made, chiefly in the southern province of Azuay, but most of the gold has been melted down.

CHAPTER SEVEN

Venezuela, the West Indies and Brazil

Art in Venezuela is virtually confined to the west and centre of the country, the areas where maize agriculture early displaced manioc cultivation. Its main expression is in pottery styles, dating between 1000 B C and the Conquest, which include figurines, but there are also stone figurines and pendants. Nowhere are there great ceremonial centres, and such ceremonial expressions as exist—shaft graves and shrines in caves—are in the west.

Among the various pottery styles a number of features recur. There are tripod bowls with the legs swollen near the top and prolonged upwards beyond the vessel rim, tetrapod bowls with modelled features representing animals, tripods or tetrapods with the feet united by a ring, vessels with ring bases pierced with holes, effigy jars with applied details, and black-on-white curvilinear painting. The Los Barrancos style, which is found in the centre and the east, where it seems to be an intrusive exception to the lack of artistic expression, has red or buff bowls with heavily flanged rims of triangular section, bearing deeply incised lines which may end in dots, and grotesquely modelled and incised head-lugs.

Most characteristic of Venezuela are vigorously modelled figurines, with more than a hint of the fantastic about them *(Ill. 247)*. The most usual subject is a woman with a head of enormously exaggerated width with curved or squared top, the latter representing a head-dress. They have applied coffee-bean eyes, breasts are rarely more than applied buttons, and the buttocks and lower limbs are excessively fat. Some are painted, generally with groups of parallel lines, in black and sometimes red on a white slip, especially in the west. Male figures without the excessive widening of the head and generally seated on a stool are also found.

246 *(opposite)* Polished stone figurine with top-knot. State of Trujillo, Venezuela

247 Pottery female figurine of characteristic Venezuelan type. State of Trujillo

There are also sexless stone figurines, some of which have excessively wide heads surmounted by a narrower top-knot, with the features and limbs ingeniously indicated by grooves and cuts. These may have a pleasing smooth convex surface *(Ill. 246)*. They are found in the west, as are wide flat sub-rectangular or V-shaped pendants of schistose material.

The West Indies seem to have been populated chiefly from Venezuela, though there are features which point in other directions. The first pottery-making, manioc-growing people spread out from the Orinoco through Trinidad and the Lesser Antilles to Puerto Rico about A D 200, carrying with them thin, well-made pottery of a pre-Barrancoid style decorated with simple white-on-red painting and incised cross-hatching, but not of great artistic interest. The Los Barrancos style followed in Trinidad and Tobago in the second half of the first millennium. Apart from this there

248 Three-pointed stone depicting a *zemi*. Puerto Rico or Eastern Santo Domingo

is little to say about the Lesser Antilles. The pottery styles of the Greater Antilles are artistically unimportant, but of greater significance are objects of stone, shell and hardwood connected with the Arawak worship of *zemis*, deities which were shown on carvings in human or animal form. One Arawak group, which lived in Puerto Rico and Hispaniola at the time of Columbus, also had a form of ceremonial centre, a rectangular or oval area bordered with rough stone slabs which may bear reliefs of *zemis*, with perishable temples for *zemi* worship at the ends. These areas were used as ball-courts, and large portable stone rings, with figure-carving perhaps representing *zemis*, are found in some. These suggest the stone yokes of the Gulf Coast of Mexico, whence the idea of both them and the game may have come. *Zemis* are also depicted on ceremonial stone celts, generally in a simple way by abrading grooves on the surface, and more elaborately on three-pointed stones which were probably a local development *(Ill. 248)*. *Zemis* were also worshipped in caves, and to this we owe the preservation of some wooden objects, not only from

39   Wooden
mi, polished and
th shell inlay,
presenting   a
ale   divinity
th   grooved
eeks. The bark
th loin-cloth is
obably a sub-
quent addition

250 Wooden stool with gold inlay on eyes, teeth and shoulders, probably representing a *zemi*. Hispaniola (Haiti or more probably Santo Domingo)

Hispaniola and Puerto Rico but also from Jamaica, which like Cuba lacked the ball-courts. From Jamaica comes a male figure with inlaid eyes and teeth of mother-of-pearl, naked except for indications of ligatures on the limbs *(Ill. 249)*, and another with a mixture of human and bird features. These and another were found in the eighteenth century and are in the British Museum, where another example, a bird with incised circles on the wings standing on a turtle, is described as from the Greater Antilles. There is also a characteristic form of narrow four-legged stool used by chiefs as a sign of rank; this dips down a little from the front which bears an animal head, probably a *zemi*, and sweeps up again to a greater height at the back. Examples are known from Jamaica, the Bahamas and Hispaniola, the last inlaid with gold. *(Ill. 250)*. Forked snuff tubes, with animal or bird heads carved on them, are known from the same contexts, and it is reported that priests used them to snuff tobacco or other narcotics from the heads of *zemis*.

BRAZIL

Little of artistic importance is known from the vast territory of Brazil; much of the area consists of lowland tropical forests which proved unsuitable for the development of high aboriginal civilizations, and those parts in the east which might be expected to be more favourable were remote and difficult of access from the main centres.

Several sites in north-east Brazil have noteworthy pottery styles, and there is another group on the Tapajós River, a tributary on the right bank of the Amazon some 300 miles from the mouth. Of the first, the most important is the Marajoara style of Marajó Island at the mouth of the Amazon, which dates from the last few centuries before the Conquest. It arrived on the island fully developed, probably from eastern Colombia or Ecuador, and declined thereafter. It is known for large burial urns, many of which are modelled in highly stylized human form, triangular female pubic coverings, and cylindrical stools, but there are many forms of bowl and jar as well. The decorative techniques are spectacular, and entire surfaces are covered with elaborate and characteristic scroll patterns. They may be painted in red or black or both on a white slip, incised on white with or without red retouching *(Ill. 252)*, scraped through a red slip showing a white one underneath *(sgraffito)*, or excised on a red-slipped vessel, the background cut away and roughened leaving the design in relief *(Ill. 251)*.

At other sites near the mouth of the Amazon, on the Maracá river, are burial urns which are much inferior in execution but

251 Two pottery vases, with brown or red slip, which has been cut away (excised) to leave the design in relief. The roughened background shows remains of whitening. Crocodile design on upper example, and sub-angular scrolls on the lower. Marajó Island, Brazil. These are relatively small examples

deserve mention as curiosities. They take the form of a human figure sitting on a bench, with the body and limbs cylindrical and the head formed by a truncated conical lid with the features applied. The presence of glass beads with some of them shows that they were being made at the time of the Conquest.

From the Tapajós river comes the style generally known as Santarém, which was being made between A D 1000 and 1500, though its full duration is unknown and the floral decoration on some tobacco pipes indicates that these at least were made under European influence. It is distinguished by its exuberant modelling and has little painting apart from the occasional use of red. Typical are jars on a flaring ring base, with the body covered with a profusion of applied detail modelled in the round with subsidiary low relief, showing animals and bird heads. They have a bulging collar which may have a human face on it, above which are one or more flanges with a short tapering spout at the top. Another characteristically extravagant form is a bowl with low vertical sides covered with modelled animal life, and supported by three or four squat human figures standing on a spool-shaped base. The eyes of both men and animals are round and bulging, and may be surrounded by a single or double raised ring. Men have mouths with swollen lips, which in the smaller instances are shown as a 'coffee bean'. On some bird heads the bulging may be so exaggerated that the eyes are on stalks, and the complexity may be increased by the placing of a knob or a head on the beak, which in many cases is curved down like the trunk of an elephant. There are also bowls covered with frogs, snakes and other details in low relief, which appear sober by comparison, although they somewhat resemble the 'witch's cauldrons' of the Milagro Phase of Ecuador, which are themselves remarkable for their exuberance. It has been suggested that the style is related to one called Arauquín in Venezuela, and that both derived elements from a common source in eastern Colombia, but, however this may be, nothing like the more elaborate types is known elsewhere and their extravagance is doubtless a local development.

252 Deep bowl with white slip, incised and retouched with red, to produce an angular S-pattern. Marajó Island, Brazil

It has only been possible to touch on the main features of the chief areas of artistic interest in ancient America, and some peoples such as the Eskimos have had to be omitted altogether, but it is hoped that enough has been said to show that art was not confined to the areas of high civilization, and that many others excelled, each in its own way. It is worth saying once again that mechanical aids were of the simplest, and that the many fine things which were made, as well as some which are more curious than beautiful, owed everything to the hand and eye of the American Indian.

Chronology

Map of Peru

Bibliography

List of Illustrations

Index

MESOAMERICA		CENTRAL MEXICO	OAXACA	GULF COAST	MAYA
POST-CLASSIC	1500	Aztec			
		Chichimec	Mixtec	Huastec	Post-Classic Maya
		Toltec	Monte Albán IV		Toltec Maya
	1000				
		Xochicalco - - - -			
CLASSIC				Classic Veracruz	
			Monte Albán III		Classic Maya
		Teotihuacán - - -			
FORMATIVE	A D / B C		Monte Albán II	Izapa style	Proto-Classic and Formative Maya
		Cuicuilco			
			Monte Albán I		
		Tlatilco		Olmec (La Venta)	
		Zacatenco			
		El Arbolillo			
	1000				
	1500				

Simplified chronological table showing the chief cultures and artistic styles mentioned in the book

THE CENTRAL ANDES	PERU					ECUADOR, COAST	N W ARGENTINA N. CHILE
	COAST			HIGHLANDS			
	NORTH	CENTRAL	SOUTH	NORTH	SOUTH		
1500 POST-CLASSIC	← The Inca Conquests →						Santa María Belén
	Chimú	Chancay	Ica				Chilean Diaguite
1000	← The Tiahuanaco Spread →				Decadent Tiahuanaco	INTEGRATION Manteño Milagro etc	
							Aguada
CLASSIC	Mochica	Interlocking	Nasca	Recuay Cursive	Tiahuanaco		
A D	Virú					REGIONAL DEVELOPMENTS	
B C					Pucára		
	Salinar		Paracas		Chiripa	Bahía Guangala, etc	
	Chavín (Cupisnique)	Chavín	Chavín	Chavín			
FORMATIVE 1000							
						FORMATIVE	
2000							
PRECERAMIC	Preceramic	Preceramic	Preceramic				
3000							

Short Bibliography

This bibliography is selective and incomplete, because the area is very un-equally covered by published work, and for large sections the only material is in the form of papers in specialist journals or privately printed. Much of this is not easily accessible and is omitted, as are books known to be out of print.

General

KELEMEN, P. *Medieval American Art.* New York, 1956

KUBLER, G. *The Art and Architecture of Ancient America.* Harmondsworth, 1962
The dating system differs in many respects from that accepted in this book

LOTHROP, S.K. *Treasures of Ancient America.* Cleveland, Ohio and London, 1964

LOTHROP, S.K., FOSHAG, W.F. and MAHLER, J. *Pre-Columbian Art : Robert Woods Bliss Collection.* New York, 1957

Mexico

CASO, A. *The Aztecs, People of the Sun.* Norman, Oklahoma, 1958

COE, M.D. *Mexico.* London, [1962]

COVARRUBIAS, M. *Indian Art of Mexico and Central America.* New York, 1957

LINNÉ, S. *Treasures of Mexican Art.* Stockholm, 1956

MARQUINA, A. *Arquitectura Prehispánica.* Mexico, 1951

Maya

MORLEY, S.G. and BRAINERD G.W. *The Ancient Maya.* Stanford, California, 1956

PROSKOURIAKOFF, T. *A Study of Classic Maya Sculpture.* Washington, 1950

RUPPERT, K., THOMPSON, J.E.S. and PROSKOURIAKOFF, T. *Bonampak, Chiapas, Mexico.* Washington, 1955

THOMPSON, J.E.S. *The Rise and Fall of Maya Civilization.* Norman, Oklahoma, 1954 and London, 1956

USA

DOCKSTADER, F.J. *Indian Art in America.* London, [1961]
This deals mainly with modern objects, but illustrates some Pre-Columbian ones

DUTTON, B.P. *Sun Father's Way: The Kiva Murals of Kuaua.* Albuquerque, 1963

MARTIN, P.S., QUIMBY, G.I. and COLLIER, D. *Indians before Columbus.* Chicago, 1947

Peru, Argentina, Chile and Ecuador

BENNET, W.C. and BIRD, J.B. *Andean Culture History,* New York, 1960

BIRD, J.B. and BELLINGER, L. *Paracas Fabrics and Nazca Needlework.* Washington, 1954

BUSHNELL, G.H.S. *Peru.* London, 1963

MASON, J. ALDEN *The Ancient Civilizations of Peru.* Harmondsworth, 1957

267

ROWE, J.H., *Chavín Art.* New York, 1962

SAWYER, A.R. *Tiahuanaco Tapestry Design.* New York, 1963

STRONG, W.D. and EVANS JR., C. *Cultural Stratigraphy in the Virú Valley.* New York, 1952

Articles in *Handbook of South American Indians*, Vol. 2. Washington, 1946
A good deal of this is out of date, but more recent material is inaccessible

Peruvian Gold. London, 1964. The catalogue of the Arts Council exhibition of part of Sr Mujica Gallo's collection

Central America, Columbia

REICHEL-DOLMATOFF, G. and A. *Colombia.* London, 1965

Articles in *Handbook of South American Indians*, Vols. 2, 4. Washington, 1946-1948

Venezuela and the West Indies

ROUSE, I. and CRUXENT, J.M. *Venezuelan Archæology.* New Haven, 1963

Articles in *Handbook of South American Indians*, Vol. 4. Washington, 1948

Brazil

Articles in *Handbook of South American Indians*, Vol. 3. Washington, 1948
When this was written, little was known of the chronology of the area. A later, work, which is concerned less with the artistic aspect than the chronology, is Meggers, B.J. and Evans C. *Archaeological Investigations at the Mouth of the Amazon.* Washington, 1957

List of Illustrations

The author and publishers are grateful to the many official bodies, institutions and individuals mentioned below for their assistance in supplying original illustration material. Abbreviations used are as follows : A M N H — American Museum of Natural History, New York; C M A E — University Museum of Archaeology and Ethnology, Cambridge; C N H M — Chicago Natural History Museum; I N A H — Instituto Nacional de Antropología, Mexico; M N A M — Museo Nacional de Antropología, Mexico; N G S — National Geographic Society. Metric measurements are given in brackets.

1 Pavement; stylized jaguar mask. Polished green serpentine slabs, coloured sands and clays. Olmec Culture, Middle Formative Period (800-400 BC). La Venta, Tabasco. About 15 ft × 25 ft (4.6× 7.6 m.). NGS. Photo Robert F. Heizer

2 Relief; figures holding were-jaguar infants. Carving on north end of Altar 5, La Venta, Tabasco. Basalt. Olmec Culture. h. of altar-stone 5 ft 1 in. (1.55 m.). NGS. Photo Matthew W. Stirling

3 Colossal head of basalt; man wearing helmet with side-flaps. Olmec Culture, Middle Formative Period. Formerly Monument 1 at La Venta, Tabasco, now in Villahermosa Park, Tabasco. h. about 8 ft (2.4 m.). Photo GHS Bushnell

4 Ceremonial group; sixteen figurines of jade and serpentine, one of conglomerate, and six jade celts, grouped possibly to show a sacrifice. Olmec Culture. Offering 4 at La Venta, Tabasco. h. of figurines between 6 5/16 in. and 7 5/16 in. (16 and 18.5). NGS. Photo Robert F. Heizer

5 Celt; figure combining delicate engraving with heavy carving. Grey-green. Olmec Culture. h. c. 1 ft (30.5). British Museum. Photo John Webb

6 Reclining infantile figurine with grimacing face; dark jade carved and drilled. Olmec Culture. Guerrero Province. AMNH

7 Carved monolith; figure with jaguar head-dress seated in the curve of a plumed rattlesnake. Basalt. Olmec Culture, Middle Formative Period (300-400 BC). Monument 19 at La Venta, Tabasco. Now at Villahermosa. Photo GHS Bushnell

8 Figurine; stylized figure with two superposed heads. Dark jade, carved and engraved. Olmec Culture, Middle Formative Period (800-400 BC). Provenance unknown h. 2 1/2 in. (6.5). Photo CMAE

9 Statue; squatting male figure, ('The Wrestler'). Basalt. Olmec Culture, Middle Formative Period. Antonio Plaza, Uxpanapa, Veracruz. h. 2 ft 2 in. (66). Private Collection. Photo Irmgard Groth-Kimball

10 Mask; human face with closed eyes and pierced ear-lobes. Wood, inlaid with jade. Olmec Cul-

ture. Said to come from a cave in the Cañon de la Mano, Iguala, Guerrero. h. 4 3/4 in. (12). AMNH

11 Figure; seated infant. White-slipped, hollow, pottery. Olmec Culture. Tlatilco, outskirts of Mexico City. h. 14 3/8 in. (36.6). Private Collection. Photo Irmgard Groth-Kimball

12 Two columns of carved glyphs; probably calendrical. Stone, low relief. Monte Albán I, Monte Albán, Oaxaca. Photo GHS Bushnell

13 Relief; Danzante; crouching human figure, with glyph near the mouth, probably a corpse. Shallow carving on sandstone revetment slab, found under later buildings. Monte Albán I, Middle to Late Formative Period. Monte Albán, Oaxaca. Photo Michael D. Coe

14 Face urn; human face with Olmecoid mouth. Polished monochrome grey ware. Monte Albán I, Middle to Late Formative Period. Monte Negro, Oaxaca. h. 6 1/8 in. (15.7). MNAM. Photo Irmgard Groth-Kimball

15 Grey pottery jar; this form with lateral spout survived into later periods. Monte Albán I. Nochistlán, Oaxaca. h. 3 1/8 in. (8). CMAE

16 Stela; shallow relief on stone showing complex scene. Stela 5, Izapa, Chiapas. Izapa Culture. Photo Brigham Young University — New World Archaeological Foundation

17 Stela and altar; shallow relief showing figure and other designs on Stela 3, Izapa, Chiapas, beneath which stands Altar 2, carved in the form of a giant toad. Izapa Culture. Photo as above

18 Head; with head-dress (fragment of pottery figurine). Modelled with incised areas and applied strips. Formative Period. Valley of Mexico. h. 3 1/8 in. (8). CMAE

19 Female figurine; Formative Period. Valley of Mexico. h. 2 3/4 in. (7). British Museum. Photo John Webb

20 Vessel; in the form of a fish. Black ware, with roughened areas originally tinted red. Formative Period. Tlatilco, Valley of Mexico. h. 5 1/4 in. (13.3). MNAM. Photo INAH

269

21 Vessel; in the form of a dog seated on its haunches. Polished black ware. Formative Period. Tlatilco, Valley of Mexico. MNAM. Photo INAH

22 Bowl; simple geometrical design. Diamonds and stripes in brown to brownish-grey, the colour of the ware, against a ground of red to dark red paint. Designs outlined by incision. Formative Period. Tlatilco, Valley of Mexico. *h.* 3 1/8 in. (18). CMAE

23 Figurine; male wearing helmet and loin-cloth. Painted pottery. Formative Period. Tlatilco, Valley of Mexico. Private Collection. Photo Irmgard Groth-Kimball

24 Figurine; female with two heads. Painted pottery with traces of black on yellow ground. Formative Period. Tlatilco, Valley of Mexico. *h.* 4 1/8 in. (10.5). Private Collection. Photo Irmgard Groth-Kimball

25 Mask; half a face, with protruding tongue, and half a skull. Light polished pottery. Formative Period. Tlatilco, Valley of Mexico. *h.* 3 1/8 in. (8). Private Collection. Photo Irmgard Groth-Kimball

26 Detail of the earlier stage of the main pyramid in the Ciudadela at Teotihuacán, Valley of Mexico. Alternating masks of the rain god and feathered serpents with rattlesnake tails and also marine shells. Teotihuacán Culture. Inner face of central pyramid in the Ciudadela. Photo Irmgard Groth-Kimball

27 Main pyramid in the Ciudadela at Teotihuacán, Valley of Mexico, which illustrates a slope-and-panel profile. Earlier stage in background. Teotihuacán Culture. Photo INAH

28 Mask; dark slate, carved and engraved. Teotihuacán Culture. Cholula. *h.* 7 5/8 in. (19.3). Private Collection. Photo Irmgard Groth-Kimball

29 Statuette; a stylized jaguar. Alabaster, carved in the round and with engraved decoration. Teotihuacán Culture. Teotihuacán, Valley of Mexico. *h.* 7 7/8 in. (20). MNAM. Photo INAH

30 Pottery stamp; mask and head-dress of the rain god. Teotihuacán I. Valley of Mexico. *w.* 1 3/8 in. (3.7). CMAE

31 Five pottery figurine heads. Heads (a) and (b) modelled, with applied elements; (c) and (d) modelled; (e) mould-made. Teotihuacán I (a) II (b) III (c and d) and IV (e). Teotihuacán region, Valley of Mexico. *h.* of (e) head 2 3/4 in. (7). CMAE

32 Tripod bowl; mask applied on the side. Negatively painted brown dots on black.

Teotihuacán, Valley of Mexico. *h.* 3 3/4 in. (9.7). CMAE

33 Jar; decorated with head of rain god, and other designs in polychrome stucco. Teotihuacán, Valley of Mexico. *h.* 6 1/4 in. (16). MNAM. Photo INAH.

34 Wide-mouthed vase; geometrical design produced by burnishing. Period II. Teotihuacán, Valley of Mexico. *h.* 4 1/2 in. (11.5). CMAE

35 Wall painting; the rain god with blue scrolls representing water, and other objects, flowing from his hands. Polychrome paint on plaster. Teotihuacán Culture. Tetitla. Photo Eugen Kusch

36 Wall painting; the rain god Tlaloc sowing, with speech scrolls emerging from his mouth. Polychrome paint on plaster. Teotihuacán Culture. MNAM. Photo GHS Bushnell

37 Wall painting; figures disporting themselves in paradise of the rain god over which he presides. Polychrome paint on plaster (partly reconstructed). Teotihuacán Culture. Painted palace at Tepantitla, Teotihuacán, Valley of Mexico. MNAM

38 Low relief; remains of facing on east side of north pyramid at Tula, showing two sets of friezes of jaguars, coyotes, eagles and monsters, separated by a slope. Formerly plastered and painted. Toltec. Tula, Hidalgo. *h.* 15 ft (4.6 m). Photo Michael D. Coe

39 Columns; square in section, with low relief carving of human figures in profile and other motifs, one carved in the round in the form of a warrior. Basalt. Toltec. Summit of north pyramid, Tula, Hidalgo. *h.* 15 ft (4.6 m.). Photo Michael D. Coe

40 Tula, Hidalgo; north Pyramid with remains of vestibule and colonnade below. Toltec. Photo GHS Bushnell

41 Bowl; Mazápan ware painted orange with composite brush on buff ground with wavy lines. Toltec. *diam.* 7 1/4 in. (18.5). CMAE

42 Vessel; in form of animal, its legs serving as supports. Plumbate with ware shell inlay. *h.* 5 3/4 in. (14.8). CMAE

43 Tripod bowl; Matlatzinca ware; red paint on cream slip. Toltec. *h.* 4 1/4 in. (10.8). CMAE

44 Extremely stylized model of a temple pyramid *(teocalli)* in carved jade. Aztec. Valley of Mexico. *h.* 1 3/4 in. (4.3). CMAE

45 Mask; the flayed god, Xipe. On the back the god is shown in the skin of a sacrificial victim. Basalt. Aztec, late 15th C. Probably Tenochtitlán, Valley of Mexico. *h.* 9 in. (22.8). British Museum. Photo Edwin Smith

46 Colossal statue; the earth goddess, Coatlicué, her severed head replaced by two snake heads, wearing a skirt of snakes and necklace of human hearts and hands. Andesite. Aztec, late 15th C. Main plaza at Tenochtitlán, Valley of Mexico. *h.* 8 ft 3 in. (2.60 m.) MNAM. Photo INAH

47 Carved stone; commemorating the victories of King Tizoc (1481-6) by showing him dressed as a god and seizing a series of captives, below glyphs naming the conquered regions. Influenced by Mixtec manuscript style. Low relief on cylindrical stone. Aztec. Main temple enclosure at Tenochtitlán, Valley of Mexico. *diam.* 8 ft 8 1/2 in. (2.75 m). MNAM. Photo INAH

48 Giant grasshopper; red stone. Aztec. Tenochtitlán, Valley of Mexico. *l.* 18 in. (45.8). MNAM. Photo INAH

49 Pendant; miniature rattlesnake, with human head in its mouth. Hard black stone veined with white. Aztec. *h.* 4 1/4 in. (11). CMAE

50 Two-tongued slit drum *(teponaztli)*; hollowed out log. Figures and glyphs intricately carved, back plain. Mixtec. Unprovenanced. *l.* 1 ft (30.5). British Museum. Photo John Webb

51 Two-tongued slit drum *(teponaztli)*; hollowed out log, carved with an owl face. Aztec. Unprovenanced. *l.* 19 in. (48). Photo Courtesy Trustees of the British Museum

52 Two-tongued slit drum *(teponaztli)*; hollowed out log, in the shape of a curly-haired canine, with dog teeth inserted. Aztec. Unprovenanced. *l.* 3 ft (91.5). MNAM. Photo INAH

53 Sacrificial knife; chalcedony blade and handle of carved wood inlaid with turquoise, malachite and shell in the form of a crouching eagle warrior. Aztec. Tenochtitlán, Valley of Mexico. *l.* 13 3/8 in. (34). Photo Courtesy Trustees of the British Museum

54 Head-dress; given by Montezuma II to Cortés. Mainly of green feathers woven and sewn onto a backing with gold ornaments. Aztec. Tenochtitlán, Valley of Mexico. *h.* over 4 ft (1.24 m). Museum für Völkerkunde, Vienna

55 Tripod bowl; with design of eagle in centre. Black paint on orange ground. Aztec III. Mexico City. *diam.* 8 in. (20.5). CMAE

56 Biconical cup; perhaps for drinking *pulque*, fermented maguey juice. Glossy red ware with dark scroll pattern. Aztec. *h.* 5 in. (12.7). CMAE

57 Spindle whorl; with engraved geometrical designs. Black pottery. Aztec. *diam.* 1 5/8 in. (4.2). CMAE

58 Figurine; perhaps goddess holding a child. Polished red pottery, mould-made. Aztec. *h.* 5 in. (12.7). Photo Courtesy Trustees of the British Museum

59 Stamp; monkey design, used for decorating textiles or the body. Red pottery. Aztec. *h.* 1 7/8 in. (4.7). CMAE

60 Relief; sacrifice of a ball-player, within a scroll frame. Classic Veracruz style. Panel of 4 stone slabs in south ball-court, El Tajín, Veracruz. Photo Michael D. Coe

61 Figurine; man dressed for the ball-game, with helmet, yoke, and *palma*. White pottery with some details picked out in black pitch. Gulf Coast. *h.* 5 in. (12.8). CMAE

62 Figurine head; pale buff pottery, eyes decorated with pitch. Classic Veracruz style. Gulf Coast. *Max. w.* 3 5/8 in. (9.2). CMAE

63 Vase; carved scroll ornament, lugs in the shape of animals. Marble. *l.* 11 in. (28). Ulua Valley, Honduras. Photo Courtesy Trustees of the British Museum.

64 *Hacha;* male head with dolphin crest. Diorite, probably, originally inlaid. Classic Veracruz culture. El Tajín, Veracruz. *h.* 11 in. (28). Private Collection. Photo Irmgard Groth-Kimball

65 Yoke; representing a stylized toad seen from above. Stone. Classic Veracruz style. Unprovenanced. *l.* about 18 in. (45.5). AMNH

66 Figurine; standing female wearing skirt and *quexquemitl*. Pale buff pottery. Eyes and other details touched in with black pitch. Classic Gulf Coast Culture. *h.* 9 in. (23). CMAE

67 'Laughing head' ; with filed teeth, wearing head-dress (fragment of a figurine). Classic Veracruz buff pottery. Gulf Coast. Max. *w.* 5 1/2 in. (14). CMAE

68 Pottery figure; seated woman wearing lip-plug with eyes and nipples painted with black pitch. A large pendant formerly hung from the necklace. *h.* 26 in. (66). From El Salto, Ignacio de la Llave, Veracruz. MNAM. Photo GHS Bushnell

271

69 'Teapot' vessel; animal head and forefeet at spout end, human head at the other, transverse handle. Black-on-cream ware. Huastec. *h.* 8 in. (20.5). British Museum. Photo John Webb

70 Bowl; inside, design of leaping animal in orange on a black ground. Post-Classic, Central Veracruz. *diam.* 7 3/4 in. (19.8). CMAE

71 Statue ('The Adolescent'); with distended ear-lobes and body partly tattooed . Carrying on his back an infant said to represent the sun. Sandstone. Huastec. Consuelo, near Tamuín, San Luis Potosí. *h.* 4 ft 4 in. (1.3 m). MNAM. Photo INAH

72 Spindle whorl; decorated in relief with two birds of prey. Cream-coloured pottery. Huastec. *diam.* 1 1/2 in. (3.9). CMAE

73 Mosaic mask; seven interlocking pieces of dark green jade, three pendants (beard) of slate, eyes and teeth of inlaid shell. Monte Albán II. Monte Albán, Oaxaca. *h.* without pendants 6 1/8 in. (15.5). MNAM. Photo INAH

74 Monte Albán, Oaxaca; general view, looking south. Site is an artificially levelled hilltop. Zapotec, Classic Period. Photo GHS Bushnell

75 Funerary urn; in the form of Cocijo, the rain god. Grey pottery. Zapotec. Monte Albán, Oaxaca. *h.* 14 1/8 in. (36). CMAE

76 Vessel; in the form of an eagle's claw. Dark grey ware. Zapotec. Monte Albán IV. Monte Albán, Oaxaca. *h.* 3 1/2 in. (9). CMAE

77 Five figurines; angular carving in jade and other hard stones. Mixtec. Some from Mitla, others unprovenanced. *h.* of tallest 1 7/8 in. (4.8). CMAE

78 Stone mosaic; in the hall adjacent to the court behind the Building of the Columns, Mitla. Mixtec. Photo GHS Bushnell

79 Woven textile; interlocking head pattern. Chimu. Peru. CMAE. Tripod vessel; interlocking head pattern, with other designs in polychrome. Mixtec. After Covarrubias

80 Tripod vessel; pottery, with white slip. Mixtec. *h.* 5 3/4 in. (14.8). CMAE

81 Vessel; Cholula Polychrome. Decorated with feathers, stone knives (in upper row) and skulls (in bottom row) and other symbols. Cholula, Puebla. *h.* 7 1/2 in. (19.2). CMAE

82 Vessel; Cholula Polychrome with a humming bird on rim. Zaachila *h.* 3 1/8 in. (8). MNAM. Photo INAH

83 Manuscript; Codex Zouche-Nuttall; part of the story of Lady Three-Flint. Pictographs painted in several colours on deerskin. Mixtec, after 1350. *h.* of page 8 in. (20.3). Facsimile; original in British Museum

84 Jewel; round shield, with step fret design and small pendant bells; behind it, four horizontal arrows. Gold, with inlay of turquoise mosaic. Mixtec. Yanhuitlán, Oaxaca. MNAM. Photo INAH

85 Pendant; four plaques in low relief and four dangling bells. Scenes on plaques are, from top to bottom; a ball game played between two gods, the solar disc, a stylized butterfly, and the Earth Monster. Gold, cast in one piece by cire perdue process. Mixtec. Tomb 7, Monte Albán, Oaxaca. *l.* 8 1/2 in. (21.6). MNAM. Photo INAH

86 Two carved spatulas; human scenes and calendar signs. Low relief on jaguar bone. Mixtec. Tomb 7, Monte Albán, Oaxaca. *l.* 7 in. (17.8).

87 Two bowls, one with tripod feet; geometrical step and chevron designs. Red and black on cream slip. Late Formative, Chupícuaro, Guanajuato. *h.* of large bowl 6 in. (15.2). CMAE

88 Figurine; solid, red pottery, with touches of red and white paints. Late Formative, Chupícuaro, Guanajuato. *h.* 4 in. (10). CMAE

89 Head; highly stylized face. Hard, dark green stone, flecked with black. Mescala or Guerrero style. *h.* 4 1/2 in. (11.7). CMAE

90 Head; face with Olmecoid features. Red pottery. Iguala, Guerrero. *h.* 2 in. (5). CMAE

91 Tripod vessel; gourd shape with narrow flared lip, feet in the form of parrots. Smoothly finished, with red slip. Colima. MNAM. Photo INAH

92 Figurine; man bound to bed. Red on yellow slip. Nayarít. *l.* 4 1/4 in. (11). CMAE

93 Vessel; gourd shape with narrow flared mouth Red slip. Nayarít. *h.* 4 3/4 in. (12). CMAE

94 Vessel; in the form of a seated hairless dog. Pottery, with red slip. Colima. *h.* 12 1/8 in. (31.1). British Museum. Photo John Webb

95 Figurine; solid buff pottery, modelled, with applied details. Colima. *h.* 6 1/2 in. (16.5). CMAE

96 Figure; man blowing conch shell. Hollow pottery, modelled, slipped. Colima. *h*. 16 in. (40.7). Arensberg Collection, Philadelphia Museum of Art

97 Corbelled vault from temple at side of ball-court. Copán, Honduras. Classic Maya. Photo GHS Bushnell

98 Ball-court at Copán, Honduras. Sloping stone sides. Classic Maya. Photo GHS Bushnell

99 Ball-court at Chichén Itzá, Yucatán. Vertical stone walls. Post-Classic Maya. Photo GHS Bushnell

100 Stela; human figure in elaborate costume and head-dress. Maya. AD 766. Stela D. Quiriguá, Guatemala. *h*. 35 ft (10.7 m.). Photo Courtesy Trustees of the British Museum, Maudslay Collection

101 Temple of the Sun at Palenque, Chiapas. General view, showing elaborate roofcomb, and façade originally covered with painted stucco. Late Classic Maya, probably dedicated in AD 692. Photo GHS Bushnell

102/3 Full-figure numerical glyphs; Part of a glyph series. Each pair of glyphs shows an era, in the form of a fantastic animal or figure, borne on the back of a number god. Low relief on limestone tablet in three sections. Late Classic Maya. Palenque, Chiapas. Photo Irmgard Groth-Kimball

104 Relief; detail of slab on the tomb under the Temple of the Inscriptions. Reclining human figure and glyphs. Low relief on limestone. Late Classic Maya. Palenque, Chiapas. Photo Eugen Kusch

105 House of the Turtles, Uxmal, Yucatán. Plain façade pierced with three doorways; fluted frieze, below, a row of small turtles. Lime concrete veneered with thin stone slabs. Late Classic Maya. Photo Eugen Kusch

106 Palace of the Governor, Uxmal, Yucatán. Façade with heavy decorated frieze pierced by two large corbelled 'arches'. Late Classic Maya, Puuc style. Photo GHS Bushnell

107 Head; young man wearing elaborate plumed head-dress. Stucco with traces of red paint. Late Classic Maya. Burial chamber under the Temple of the Inscriptions, Palenque, Chiapas, (i.e. the same chamber as *Ill. 104*). *h*. 15 3/8 in. (39). MNAM. Photo Irmgard Groth-Kimball

108 Bowl; marine monsters and stylized glyphs. Orange and black on buff slip. Late Classic Maya. Caracol, British Honduras. *h*. 3 1/2 in. (9). CMAE

109 Design on vase; scene with priests and dignitaries in full costume. Red, yellow and black paint on buff slip. Late Classic Maya. Chama, Guatemala. *h*. about 9 in. (23). Cary Collection, The University Museum, Philadelphia. Painting by M. Louise Baker

110 Wall painting; raid on an inferior tribe to get prisoners. Polychrome paint on plaster (perhaps true fresco). Maya, *c*. AD 800. Bonampak, Chiapas. Copy by Antonio Tejeda. The Peabody Museum, Harvard University

111 Vase; kneeling figures with head-dresses, above a band of glyphs. Polychrome. Classic Maya. AMNH

112 Tripod bowl with cover; incised designs, including bird which is also modelled on the cover. Early Classic Maya, from the painted tomb at Tikal, Guatemala. AD 457. The University Museum, Philadelphia

113 Whistle figurine; seated man wearing elaborate plumed head-dress. Grey pottery, mould-made, the necklace painted blue. Late Classic Maya. Jaina, Campeche. CMAE

114 Figurine; female wearing ear-spools and necklace. Red ware with touches of red and white, modelled. with applied details. Formative Maya. *h*. 7 in, (18). CMAE

115 Plaque; seated dignitary or god wearing elaborate head-dress. Pale green jade, carved and drilled in low relief and highly polished. Classic Maya. Unprovenanced. *l*. 3 in. (7.7). British Museum. Photo John Webb

116 Large annular flare; four glyphs on plain surface. Ear-spool shape, but perhaps a belt ornament. Dark green jade, engraved and highly polished. Proto-Classic Maya (Late Formative.). Pomona, Bristish Honduras. *diam*. 7 in. (17.8). British Museum. Photo Eileen Tweedy

117 Eccentric flint; flaked to incorporate human profiles. Perhaps head of ceremonial staff. Maya. Unprovenanced. *l*. 10 in. (25.4). Photo Courtesy Trustees of the British Museum

118 El Castillo, Chichén Itzá, Yucatán. General view of pyramid crowned with a temple. Post-Classic Maya. Photo Eugen Kusch

119 Relief; human skulls on poles. Shallow relief on the *tzompantli* or skull rack. Post-Classic Maya. Chichén Itzá, Yucatán. Photo GHS Bushnell

120 Pillar; in the form of a feathered serpent, its rattlesnake tail formerly supporting lintel of the temple entrance. Post-Classic Maya. Temple of the

Warriors, Chichén Itzá, Yucatán. Photo GHS Bushnell

121 Wall painting; a waterside village (copy), showing various activities and canoes carrying warriors. Polychrome on plaster. Post-Classic Maya, 12th C. Temple of the Warriors, Chichén Itzá, Yucatán *h.* 9 ft×12 1/2 ft (2.75 m.×3.83 m.). Copy by A. Axtell Morris, courtesy The Peabody Museum, Harvard University

122 Five ornaments; geometrical forms, including scrolls and a swastika. Native copper, cut, beaten and annealed. Hopewell Culture, Ohio. CNHM

123 Three tobacco pipes; bowls in the form of marmot, frog, and snake; front views show smoke channel. Steatite, carved, with some shell inlay. Hopewell Culture, Ohio. *l.* of frog pipe, 3 3/8 in. (9.2). Photo Courtesy Trustees of the British Museum

124 Two silhouettes; mutilated human figures. Thin sheet of mica. Hopewell Culture, Ohio

125 Two silhouettes; human hand and eagle claw. Thin sheet of mica. *l.* of eagle claw *c.* 10 in. (25.4). Hopewell Culture, Ohio. CNHM

126 Mask; deer head, with large leather-hinged ears. Carved wood, originally painted. Late Prehistoric. Key Marco, Florida. *l.* 10 3/4 in. (27.5). University Museum, Philadelphia.

127 Bottle; swirl design. Pottery, painted red and white. Middle Mississippi Period, after AD 1000. Child's grave at Halcombs Mounds, Arkansas. Peabody Museum, Harvard University

128 Bottle; concentric linear designs. Pottery with burnished black slip, incised after firing; traces of red paint in incisions. Caddo. Middle Mississippi Period, after AD 1000. Lafayette County, Arkansas. Museum of the American Indian, Haye Foundation

129 Bowl; black on white, showing contrast between areas of solid colour and hatching. Pueblo III, *c.* AD 1050-1300. Mesa Verde, Colorado. *diam.* 10 in. (25.4). British Museum. Photo Edwin Smith

130 Coiled burden basket; geometrical design in red and black on natural ground. Basketmaker III Period AD 500-700, Canyon del Muerto, Arizona. *diam.* 32 in. (82.) University of Colorado Museum

131 Bowl; stylized turtle within geometrical border. Black paint on white slip. A hole has been punched in the centre, ceremonially 'killing' the bowl for burial with the dead. AD 1000-1200. Swarts Ranch, Mimbres Valley, New Mexico. *diam.* 10 1/2 in. (27.) Peabody Museum, Harvard University

132 Fragment of bowl; Sikyatki Polychrome. Painted in black and red on yellow. Ruin 4, Horn House, Moki Reservation, Arizona. Peabody Museum, Harvard University

133 Vase; geometrical and scroll designs in compartments. Black and red paint on buff slip. *c.* AD 1300-1450. Chihuahua, Mexico. *h.* 8 in. (20.5). CMAE

134 Design; extended pattern on carved gourd *(Ill. 135).* Preceramic Period. Huaca Prieta, Chicama Valley, Peru. Drawing Courtesy the AMNH, New York

135 Carved gourd vessel with cover; Preceramic Period, *c.* 2000 BC. Huaca Prieta, Chicama Valley. *diam. c.* 2 3/8 in. (6). AMNH

136 Twined textile; design indicated only by direction of warp displacement. Cotton. Preceramic Period. Chicama Valley. *l.* 8 1/2 in. (21.5). By kind permission of AMNH

137 Twined textile; condor with snake in its stomach. *(Ill. 136)* after analysis with design plotted and superposed. By kind permission of AMNH

138 Annular vessel with stirrup spout; on ring, two human heads and two heads combining bird (probably owl)) and feline features yellowish-grey ware. Cupisnique (Coast Chavín) style. North Coast. *h.* 8 in. (20.5). Royal Scottish Museum

139 Carved monolith; upper section of the Great Image. Human figure with feline fangs and snakes as hair. White granite. Chavín Culture, probably 9th C. BC. Old temple block, Chavín de Huántar. Total height nearly 15 ft (4.58 m.). Rubbing by Fred D. Ayres, courtesy the Museum of Primitive Art, New York

140 Frieze; stylized birds with feline jaws and eyes and snake heads. Chavín Culture. Lintel of the black and white portal, temple at Chavín de Huántar. Rubbing. Photo Abraham Guillén

141 Low relief; bird decorated with feline heads in profile. Chavín Culture. Temple at Chavín de Huántar. Photo Abraham Guillén

142 Two engraved slabs; left, human figure with severed legs; right, trophy head. Chavín Period. Part of retaining wall of temple platform at Cerro Sechín, Casma Valley. Photo Hans Mann

143 Circular gold repoussé plaque; feline face with snake head appendages, within guilloche border. Late Chavín style. Possibly from Chavín de Huántar. *diam.* 4 13/16 in. (12.2). Bliss Collection, Dumbarton Oaks (Trustees for Harvard University)

274

144 Mortar; in the shape of a jaguar, with stylized markings. Stone, carved in the round and incised. Eyes originally inlaid. Chavín Culture. *l.* 13 in. (33). The University Museum, Philadalphia

145 Bottle; monochrome, dark-coloured, with incised feline-inspired designs surrounded by rocker stamping. Cupisnique style. Courtesy Rafael Larco Hoyle

146 Stirrup-spouted jar; dark monochrome pottery, with rough surface perhaps suggested by a spondylus shell. Early Cupisnique style. Courtesy Rafael Larco Hoyle

147 Stirrup-spouted jar; in the form of a woman suckling a child. Dark pottery. Cupisnique style. Courtesy Rafael Larco Hoyle

148 Stirrup-spouted vessel; in the form of a modelled monkey standing on annular base. Reddish-brown ware. Salinar Culture, later centuries BC. Chicama Valley. Courtesy Rafael Larco Hoyle

149 Spout and bridge vessel; spout balanced by human head with closed eyes, wearing cap. Modelled with simple, black linear negative painting on red ground. Gallinazo (Virú) style. Virú Valley. *h.* 6 in. (15). CMAE

150 Spout and bridge vessel; warrior carrying club and shield on reed raft. Negative painting. Gallinazo (Virú) style. Early Classic. Virú Valley. Courtesy Rafael Larco Hoyle

151 Bowl; fish alternating with decorative panels. Pottery, with pressed relief, painted in red and white. Mochica. *h.* 4 3/4 in. (12). CMAE

152 Stirrup-spouted pottery vessel; in the shape of a house with open porch. Painted in red and white. Mochica. Linden-Museum, Stuttgart

153 Effigy vessel with stirrup spout; in the form of a seated man wearing a cap. Incised and with some scraped areas (stripes on cap), highly burnished red slip. Early Mochica. *h.* 6 3/4 in. (17.1). Photo Courtesy Trustees of the British Museum

154 Stirrup-spouted jar; drummer wearing bird mask and wings. Painted in red and white. Late Mochica. *h.* 11 3/4 in. (29.9). British Museum. Photo John Webb

155 Stirrup-spouted jar; a warrior and his dog chase a spotted deer with a club, with the three-dimensional figure of a deer on top of the vessel. Modelled and painted in red and white. Mochica. *h.* 9 1/2 in. (24.2). British Museum. Photo John Webb

156 Spatula handle; in the form of an arm, with engraved figure of a warrior dressed as a bird, and inset turquoise and pyrite nodules. The blade is plain. Mochica. Santa Valley. *l.* 8 1/4 in. (21). British Museum. Photo John Webb

157 Wooden head of copper-shod ceremonial digging-stick; shell and turquoise inlay. Shows a tusked figure holding a digging-stick and accompanied by a boy. Found in the grave of an old man and a boy similarly dressed, at Huaca de la Cruz, Virú Valley. Mochica. After WD Strong

158 Portrait vase; head of a man with painted face wearing cap and ear-spools. White and red. Mochica. *h.* 6 1/4 in. (16). Collection Dr MGM Pryor

159 Portrait vase with stirrup spout; head of a man with painted face wearing a decorated cap. Painted in red and white. Mochica. *h.* 11 5/8 in. (29.6). British Museum. Photo John Webb

160 Gold puma skin with three dimensional head; on the animal's tongue a human face appears and on its body a design of double two-headed serpents. The belly in two thicknesses forms a pouch. Gold repoussé work and wire. Mochica. *l.* 24 5/8 in. (62.5). M. Mugica Fallo Collection. Photo John Webb

161 Jar; with flange mouth, and lateral spout above a modelled human head between two animals. Decorated with black negative painting over white and red, illustrating a crested jaguar and other features. Recuay style, Callejón de Huaylas, North Highlands. *h.* 7 1/8 in. (20). CMAE

162 Bowl and two sherds; cursive scroll pattern, including stylized faces and animals. Colours vary from red-brown to black, with some grey on cream ground. Cajamarca, North Highlands. *diam.* of dish 4 3/4 in. (12.5). CMAE

163 Spout and bridge vessel; spout balanced by stylized bird's head. Surface burnished except for head and large feline face at one end. Some details picked out in red after firing. Paracas style, Formative Period. South Coast. *h.* 7 1/4 in. (18). CMAE

164 Double spout and bridge vessel; buff with incised decoration suggesting matting on body and bridge. Parts picked out in red, yellow, black and white resinous paint, applied after firing. Paracas style, Formative Period. South Coast. *h.* 5 1/2 in. (14). CMAE

165 Spout and bridge effigy jar; modelled to represent a woman and painted in black, white, dark red, yellow and orange. Nasca style, Classic Period. South Coast. *h.* 6 1/4 in. (16). CMAE

275

166 Spout and bridge vessel; represents a jaguar. Burnished black. The markings are incised and most of the surface was probably originally covered with resinous post-fired colours of which some red, yellow, grey and white remains. Paracas style, Formative Period. South Coast. *h.* 5 7/8 in. (15). CMAE

167 Double spout and bridge vessel; two rows of crabs. Red, orange and dark grey paint on black over dark red slip. Early Nasca, Classic Period. *h.* 7 in. (17.8). British Museum. Photo John Webb

168 Beaker; painted in red, purplish red, grey, yellow and black on white ground showing a demon between inner bands of geometrical design and outer ones of trophy heads. Late Nasca, Classic Period. South Coast. *h.* 7 7/8 in. (20). CMAE

169 Textile; part of border of mantle covered with solid alpaca wool embroidery showing outlines of small cats within larger ones. Paracas *w.* 4 1/4 in. (11). CMAE

170 Tapestry textile; rare type, in rose pink, light blue and yellow, with design showing a stylized monster worked in small beads strung on the warp. Nasca. *w.* of design 6 1/4 in. (15.5). CMAE

171 Clothing; lay figure dressed in richly embroidered mantle, turban and undergarments. Textiles from a Paracas mummy. National Museum, Lima. Photo Courtesy Dr Jorge Muelle

172 Markings on barren plateau above the Nasca Valley. Linear patterns have been formed by removing surface pebbles to expose the yellow sandy soil. Nasca Culture. Photo Hans Mann

173 Bowl; with feline head and tail and wavy rim, painted in red, black, white, orange and brown on pale brown ware. Early Tiahuanaco, Formative Period. South Highlands. *h.* 4 3/4 in. (12). CMAE

174 Beaker *(kero)*; upper band of stylized heads, lower of stylized felines, all in profile. Polychrome paint on red slip. Classic Tiahuanaco. *h.* 6 1/2 in. (16.5). The University Museum, Philadelphia

175 Relief; central figure from monolithic doorway holding staves. Tiahuanaco, Bolivia. Classic Period. Size of gate 12 ft×10 ft (3.76×3.5 m.). Photo Abraham Guillén

176 Statue; kneeling male, wearing head-dress. Limestone. Late Formative Period. Pokotía, near Tiahuanaco, Bolivia. Photo Abraham Guillén

177 Statue; figure wearing loin-cloth and cap and carrying a human head. Stone. Late Formative

Period. Pucára, South Highlands, Peru. Photo Abraham Guillén

178 Potsherd; stylized feline head with vertically divided eyes. Design in low relief incised and painted in black and red. Late Formative Period. Pucára, South Highlands, Peru. Max. *w.* 10.2 3/4 in. (7). CMAE

179 Poncho shirt; with vertical bands of tapestry bearing abstract designs. The vertically divided eyes show the derivation from Tiahuanaco. Coast Tiahuanaco, Early Post-Classic Period. The Textile Museum, Washington

180 Process of stylization; from falcon-headed, staff-bearing attendant figure on the monolithic gateway, Tiahuanaco, to textile designs, Coast Tiahuanaco Culture. Drawings by Milton Franklin Sonday, Jr., from Alan R. Sawyer, *Tiahuanaco Tapestry Design*, 1963. Courtesy The Museum of Primitive Art, N.Y.

181 Cap; square, with peaked corners and geometrical decoration. Knotted pile cloth, wool, in red, turquoise, blue, buff, brown and white. Coast Tiahuanaco, Early Post-Classic Period. Each side 5×3 in. (12.7×7.6). Photo Courtesy Trustees of the British Museum

182 Double spout and bridge vessel; falcon-headed, staff-bearing figure with wings. Polychrome Coast Tiahuanaco Culture. *h.* 6 in. (15.2). British Museum. Photo John Webb

183 Bowl; with animal head, rudimentary limbs and tail in relief, painted with geometrical designs in black, white and red. End of Coast Tiahuanaco Period. *h.* 4 3/4 in. (12). CMAE

184 Face-collar jar; on neck, head of man wearing hat and ear-spools, on body, felines in pressed relief. Painted in washy black, white and orange on buff ground. Late North Coast Tiahuanaco style. *h.* 7 1/2 in. (19). CMAE

185 Relief; on wall in the fortress of Chan Chan. Bands of birds, fish, and fantastic animals, and of scrolls and step ornament. Moulded mud-plaster. Chimú Culture. Later Post-Classic. Photo Hans Mann

186 Double spout and bridge ceremonial vessel; ornamental band on body, openwork crest on bridge, free-standing elements in the form of two monkeys and four heads. Hammered silver. Chimú. Lambayeque Valley. *h.* 7 2/8 in. (20). M. Mugica Gallo Collection. Photo John Webb

187 Drinking vessel *(Paccha)*; in the form of a man fishing from a reed raft. Black ware. Chimú. *l.* 12 1/4 in. (31). CMAE

188 Canteen; with pressed relief of jaguar on body, and two small handles. Black ware. Chimú. *h*. 9 in. (23). CMAE

189 Stirrup-spouted vessel with monkey on spout; man holding a child on a cubical base. Black ware. Against background of contemporary textile with brocaded fish and pelican designs. Chimú. CMAE

190 Beaker; standing male figure with, plumed head-dress and ear-spools, holding staves. Repoussé gold. Head-dress and ear-spools inlaid with turquoise. Chimú. Lambayeque Valley. *h*. 7 7/8 in. (20). M. Mugica Gallo Collection. Photo John Webb

191 Funerary mask; face with ear and nose ornaments. Gold, with stone eyes and traces of red and green paint. Chimú. Lambayeque Valley. *w*. 22 3/8 in. (57). M. Mugica Gallo Collection. Photo John Webb

192 Ear-spool; reversible design of two birds with a common body. Wood, with crenellated and polished edge, inlaid with coloured shell. Chimú. *diam*. 1 7/8 in. (4.7). British Museum. Photo John Webb

193 Ear-spools; central head with head-dress, surrounded by 10 similar heads. Thin silver, repoussé, Chimú. *diam*. 5 1/2 in. (14). AMNH

194 Ceremonial knife; blade with semi circular cutting-edge surmounted by the hollow figure of a deer, and danglers. Blade of base metal with gold plating, ornaments of gold. Chimú. Lambayeque Valley. *h*. 12 13/16 in. (30). M. Mugica Gallo Coll. Photo John Webb

195 Painted plain weave textile; fantastic faces in compartments separated by scrolls and chevrons. Designs in brown on buff ground originally white. Painted designs at this time show far less sureness of touch than woven ones. Chimú. Each panel. *c*. 2 3/4 in. (7) square. CMAE

196 Double cloth with design of pelicans in brown and white (below), and border of tapestry worked on gauze with pelicans within scrolled lozenges. Chimú. Size of detail shown 10 1/4 in. × 16 in. (26×41). CMAE

197 Doll; representing fisherman and net. Slit tapestry face and warp-striped plain weave shirt. In pink, white, black, buff, yellow, green and pale lavender. Chancay Valley, Central Coast. *h*. 9 1/2 in. (24). CMAE

198 Warp striped textile; pattern of brocaded cats in blue, yellow and brown on dirty white. Chimú. *h*. 10 1/4 in.× 10 1/4 in (24×24). CMAE

199 Large ovoid jar. Black-on-white decoration. Chancay style, Later Post-Classic. Central Coast. *h*. 17 in. (43.3). Photo Courtesy Trustees of the British Museum

200 Three bowls; all with textile-inspired designs in black, white and red. Ica style, Later Post Classic. South Coast. *h*. of largest 6 in. (15.2). Photo Courtesy Trustees of the British Museum

201 Machu Picchu; general view, showing low semi-circular tower. Inca, after 1450. Photo Hans Mann

202 Saccsaihuamán, Cuzco; lowest wall of zig-zag rampart of the fortress. Irregular 'megalithic' masonry. Inca, mid 15th C. Photo Nicholas Young

203 Statuette; alpaca with a hole in its back. Hard black stone. Inca. *l*. 4 in. (1 ·.2). British Museum. Photo John Webb

204 Jar with lugs; polychrome with geometrical designs and snakes, lugs in the form of jaguars. Inca, after 1450. Region of Cuzco. Museo Arqueológico, Cuzco. Photo Abraham Guillén

205 Provincial aryballus; stylized plant design in black and white, the base red. Chile. *h*. 10 5/8 in. (27). CMAE

206 Provincial aryballus; with a pressed relief. Black ware. Chimú-Inca style. North Coast. After Inca conquest (*c*. 1470). *h*. 7 1/2 in. (19). CMAE

207 Aryballus; Cuzco polychrome decorated with geometrical pattern. Inca, after 1450. Photo Courtesy Trustees of the British Museum

208 Vessel with one handle; painted black, white and orange. Inca-Ica style. Ica Valley, South Coast. After the Inca conquest (*c*. 1480). *h*. 3 7/8 in. (10). CMAE

209 Poncho shirt; geometrical and feather designs, two small human figures within characteristic V neck. Vicuña wool tapestry. Inca. From an island in Lake Titicaca. AMNH

210 Statuette; llama with saddle blanket and girth. Cast silver with gold appliqué. Red cinnabar-resin inlay of saddle blanket restored. Inca. *h*. 9 1/8 in. (23.2). AMNH

211 Santa Maria funerary urn; stylized face on neck. Black and red paint on cream slip. Catamarca and neighbouring provinces, North West Argentina. After A D 1000. *h*. 21 1/2 in. (54.8). British Museum. Photo John Webb

277

212 Bowl; stylized face and linear designs. Red, white, and grey. Chilean diaguite. Near Coquimbo, North Coast of Chile. Late Period, after A D 1000. CMAE

213 Four tablets and two tubes for taking snuff; human and animal motifs. Atacameño region, Rio Loa area, North Coast of Chile. AMNH

214 Plaque; human figure between two felines. Copper, cast by cire perdue process. Aguada Culture, A D 700-1000. North West Argentina. *w.* 6 1/4 in. (16). CMAE

215 Statue; seated male figure eating maize cob, Lava. Highland Costa Rica. *h.* 6 1/2 in. (16.5). CMAE

216 *Metate*; slab for grinding corn, in the form of an animal. Stone. Costa Rica. *l.* 16 in. (41). CMAE

217 Miniature stool; stone. Province of Chiriquí, Panama. *h.* 3 1/2 in. (9). CMAE

218 Celt; angular human head and arms carved on upper half, blade ground to fine edge. Greygreen jade. Nicoya, Costa Rica. *l.* 4 7/8 in. (12.4). British Museum. Photo John Webb

219 Pendant; bird with snake appendages. Gold, cast by cire perdue process. Veraguas Province, Panama. *h.* and *w.* 4 in. (10.2). Fitzwilliam Museum, Cambridge

220 Tripod bowl; with animal's heads as feet. Nicoya. Polychrome pottery. Pacific Coast of Costa Rica. *h.* 5 in. (12.5). CMAE

221 Globular vessel with lugs; Alligator Ware. Two alligators sharing a central body within striped border, lugs modelled as animal heads. Black, red and white. Chiriquí, Panama. *h.* 7 1/2 in. (19). CMAE

222 Globular vessel; black negative painting over white and red. Chiriquí, Panama. *h.* 4 in. (10.5). CMAE

223 Quadrangular tripod bowl; with animal head and tail. Painted in black, white and red. Highland Polychrome ware. Costa Rica. *h.* 3 1/4 in. (8.5). CMAE

224 Figurine; squatting woman wearing brassière. Black, white and red. Nicoya Polychrome. Pacific Coast of Costa Rica. *h.* 6 1/2 in. (16.5). CMAE

225 Ovoid tripod vase; applied animal head on side, the forelegs forming two of the vessel's feet.

Painted in red, black and white. Nicoya Polychrome. Pacific Coast of Costa Rica. *h.* 11.2 in. (28.6). Photo Courtesy Trustees of the British Museum

226 Pedestal dish; characteristic pointed hooks and crocodile heads in red, black, white and purple. Coclé, Panama. *diam.* 11 1/2 in. (29). CMAE

227 Bottle; black, red and purple on cream. Coclé, Panama. *h.* 5 1/2 in. (13.5). CMAE

228 Statue; fanged human figure wearing cap and loin-cloth, and carrying staff and shield. Coarse stone. San Agustín, Colombia. *h.* about 4 ft (1.20 m.). Photo Courtesy Trustees of the British Museum

229 Shaft grave; view of interior. Stone, walls painted in several colours. Tierradentro region, Cauca, Colombia. *After G. Kubler,* 1962

230 Figurine *(tunjo)*; flat, human figure with wiry details wearing head-dress, carrying staff and shield. Gold cast by cire perdue process. Chibcha, Colombia, *h.* 2 1/2 in. (6.2). CMAE

231 Three objects of precious metal; bell-shaped piece of uncertain use, decorated with a row of faces, gourd-shaped flask, and seated female figurine. Outer objects of *tumbaga* (gold-copper alloy), central one of gold. Quimbaya, Cauca Valley, Colombia. *h.* of flask *c.* 4 in. (10.2). Photo Courtesy Trustees of the British Museum

232 Bowl; pattern of geometrical areas and spots. Black negative painting over red. Quimbaya, Colombia. *h.* 3 3/4 in. (9.5). CMAE

233 Bowl; parts of surface cut away in champlevé technique. Red ware. Quimbaya, Colombia. *h.* 3 1/8 in. (8). CMAE

234 Head; with head-band, ear ornaments, and necklace stamped and incised. Pottery. Chibcha, Colombia. *h.* 13/16 in. in. (19.9). British Museum. Photo John Webb

235 Head; with elaborate head-dress, ear ornaments, and necklace stamped and incised. Pottery. Chibcha, Colombia. Max. *w.* 3 1/4 in. (8). CMAE

236 Statue; standing male figure wearing a cap and belt with two pendant strips. Manteño Phase, Integration Period. Manabí Province, coast of Ecuador. *h.* 4 ft (1.20 m.). CMAE

237 Bat; dolerite slightly shaped and incised. Manteño Phase, Integration Period. La Libertad, Guayas, coast of Ecuador. *w.* 8 3/4 in. (22). CMAE

278

238 Two vessels; simple forms with traces of iridescent paint and highly polished. Formative Period. La Libertad, Guayas, coast of Ecuador. *h.* of larger vessel 3 1/2 in. (9). CMAE

239 Three painted sherds; *(top left)* chocolate on yellow, Guangala, *(top right)* stylized pelicans in red and black on yellow, La Libertad, *(belom)* red and black on yellow, La Libertad. Guangala Phase, Regional Development Period. Province of Guayas, coast of Ecuador. CMAE

240 Figurine; standing male, wearing ear-spools and nose-ring. Grey pottery. Manteño Phase. Integration Period. La Libertad, Guayas, Ecuador. *h.* 5 1/4 in. (13). CMAE

241 Stone-coloured pottery figurine; standing woman wearing domed hat. Bahía Phase, Regional Development Period. Esmeraldas, coast of Ecuador. *h.* 5 1/2 in. (14). CMAE

242 Hollow whistle figurine; standing male, wearing swept-back domed hat and holding a child. Red-brown largely smoked to dark grey pottery. Guangala Phase, Regional Development Period. Guangala, Guayas, coast of Ecuador. *h.* 12 1/4 in. (31.5). CMAE

243 Face-collar urn; limbs indicated by burnishing, face with heavy applied eyebrows and fangs. Grey-brown ware. Manteño Phase, Integration Period. Salinas, Guayas, coast of Ecuador. *h.* 17 in. (43). CMAE

244 Pottery figurine head; wearing domed hat, ear-spools and nose-ring. Bahía Phase, Regional Development Period. Said to be from Esmeraldas, but probably from Manabí, coast of Ecuador. Photo Hans Mann

245 Bowl; on low ring base. Black negative decoration showing outlines of two animals over red and cream.

Tuncahuán style, El Angel, Province of Carchi, North Highlands of Ecuador. *diam.* 8 1/4 in. (21). CMAE

246 Figurine; sexless, with topknot. Stone, grooved and polished. State of Trujillo, Venezuela. Department of Anthropology, Caracas. Photo Bela Sziklay. Courtesy Professor JM Cruxent

247 Pottery female figurine; characteristic Venezuelan type. State of Trujillo. Department of Anthropology. Caracas. Photo Bela Sziklay. Courtesy Professor JM Cruxent

248 Three-pointed stone; depicting a *zemi*. Puerto Rico or Eastern Santo Domingo. Length 9 in. (23). CMAE

249 *Zemi*; representing standing male divinity with grooved cheeks. The bark cloth loin-cloth probably a subsequent addition. Carved and polished wood with shell inlay. Carpenters Mountain, Jamaica. *h.* 3 ft 5 in. (1.4 m). British Museum. Photo John Webb

250 Stool with high back; in the form of a fantastic creature with human head. Wood, carved and incised, with gold inlay on eyes, teeth and shoulders. Hispaniola (Haiti or more probably Santo Domingo) *l.* 17 in. (43). British Museum. Photo John Webb

251 Two vases; alligators and abstract all-over designs. Pottery with brown or red slip with background excised from the design leaving it in relief. Marajó Island, Brazil. *h.* 8 5/8 in. (22) and 9 in. (23). The University Museum, Philadelphia

252 Deep bowl; white slip incised and retouched with red to produce angular S-pattern. Marajó Island, Brazil. *h.* 12 1/2 in. (32). The University Museum, Philadelphia

The maps for the book were drawn by Shalom Schotten

Map of Mexico showing the most important sites

Cocle

Quimbaya

Calima

TOLIMA

Bogotá

TIERRADENTRO

ESMERALDAS · San Agustín

· Esmeraldas

Manta

MANABI

Guayas

Guayaquil

GUAYAS

Marañón

Amazon

Cajamarca

Huamachuco

Lambayeque
Jequetepeque
Cupisnique
Chicama
Moche
Santa
Viru
Nepeña
Santa
Fortaleza

Callejón de Huaylas

NORTH
HIGHLANDS

Chavin

Chan Chan

Supe

Kotosh CENTRAL
HIGHLANDS

Chancay

Huaylas

MANTARO
BASIN

Unubamba

Ancón

Lima

Rimac

Lurin

Pachacámac

Asia

Huari

Machu Picchu

Cuzco

SOUTH
HIGHLANDS

Chincha

Pisco

Ica

Pucára

LAKE TITICACA

Sillustani

Chiripa

Peninsula of Paracas

Nasca

Tiahuanaco

Cochabamba

CATAMARCA

LA RIOJA

p of Peru showing the most important sites.

287

Thi~ b   ~r

THE WORLD OF ART LIBRARY

Details of paperback editions of this series can
be obtained from your bookseller

THAMES AND HUDSON

30 Bloomsbury Street, London, W.C.1